T0303167

Worship Musician!

Presents

THE WORSHIP VOCAL BOOK

THE WORSHIP VOCAL BOOK

The Modern Worship Singer's Complete Guide to Developing Technique, Style, and Expression

Tim Carson

Hal Leonard Books
An Imprint of Hal Leonard Corporation

Published in 2013 by Hal Leonard Books
An Imprint of Hal Leonard Corporation
7777 West Bluemound Road
Milwaukee, WI 53213

Trade Book Division Editorial Offices
33 Plymouth St., Montclair, NJ 07042

All images, except 4.12 and 4.13, from Dreamstime
Music graphics and images 4.12 and 4.13 courtesy of Bill Gibson

Video produced by Gummi Ibsen, www.gummibsen.com

Printed in the United States of America

Book design by Mayapriya Long, Bookwrights

Library of Congress Cataloging-in-Publication Data is available upon request.

ISBN 9781458443205

www.halleonardbooks.com

This book is dedicated to Dr. Ronald Combs:
Thank you for your coaching, for believing and encouraging, and for so openly sharing your wealth of knowledge and talent. You are a gift.

Contents

Introduction

I have been coaching singers for over 20 years. The singers I have worked with represent a wide range of experience, natural talent, and ability. Some of them earn their paycheck with their voice, some are brand-new beginners when they walk into my voice studio, and there's a wide continuum in between. Their motivations for knocking on my door also vary significantly. Some want to increase their vocal range, some want to train their voices to sing in different styles, and some come to me with significant vocal damage, having abused their voices through misuse—it's my job to try to patch them up and get them back on the road.

While these differences seem vast, there is an overarching commonality for all of these singers that has to do with the heart. On a much deeper level than the desire to simply sound good, or sing higher or louder, is a passion to more fully express the heart through the voice. But all the singers who have ever walked through my door experience vocal limitations that keep them from conveying the full palette of feelings and experiences that they long to communicate through song.

They know the way their hearts were engaged on Sunday morning as they led worship. But when they listen to a recording of the service, there's a gap where their voices couldn't express the depth of their hearts. Many of these singers have simply resigned themselves to the belief that this will always be the case for them. There is so much more that they want to express from their hearts, but they feel stuck playing the hand that they've been dealt.

The good news is that singing is a learnable skill! It's why I am in the business I am in. I have had a front row seat for over 20 years now as thousands of singers have discovered newfound freedom, strength, and style to express their hearts through song. I am convinced that this growth is available to every singer who is willing to do the hard work required. This book outlines a strategy and game plan for the worship singer who wants to develop his or her full vocal potential.

I am in the business of doing something much more profound than helping singers sound pretty. I am in the business of unleashing hearts—a journey that involves more than just a singer's voice box, but all of who he or she is to the very core of the soul. It's an amazing journey for those who are dedicated and courageous enough to walk down the path. You are invited to this great adventure, and I welcome you to join us as we explore one of God's greatest gifts to humanity—the ability to sing!

THE WORSHIP VOCAL BOOK

1

The Instrument You Play

As a singer you play the most intricately designed instrument on the planet. It is unmatched by any other instrument in its versatility and complexity, and by the fact that it is an organic, living structure. The voice, the way it works, and what we are capable of doing with it are nothing short of miraculous. Before we get into developing your ability to sing, let's take a quick peek at what's under the hood and find out a little bit about how this instrument is designed.

The Structure of the Larynx

The instrument you play as a singer is called the larynx, or voice box. The main structure of the larynx is made up of three cartilages: the thyroid cartilage, the cricoid cartilage, and a pair of arytenoid cartilages. The largest of the cartilages is the *thyroid cartilage*. The thyroid cartilage is a large, shield-like cartilage that sits at the forward-facing side of the larynx. It is the structure that we feel and see in the male Adam's apple as it protrudes slightly in front of the rest of the throat. The female thyroid cartilage is located in exactly the same place but is not as easily recognizable because it is a fraction of the size of the male larynx.

The structure of the larynx sits on the *cricoid cartilage*, a signet ring–shaped cartilage—a cylinder that is smaller at the front (under the thyroid cartilage) and larger in the back.

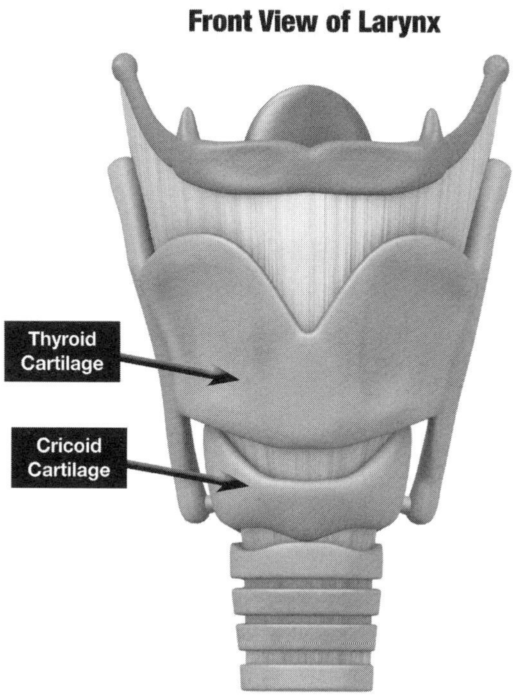

Figure 1.1. Thyroid Cartilage and Cricoid Cartilage (Front View)

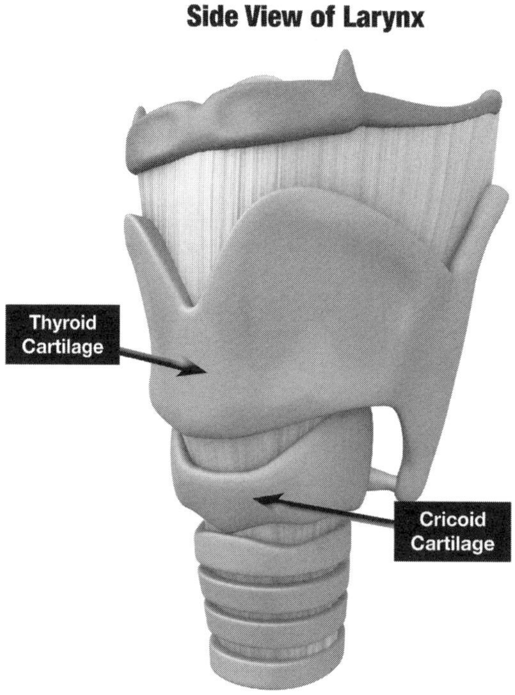

Figure 1.2. Thyroid Cartilage and Cricoid Cartilage (Side View)

The final structure of the larynx is the pair of *arytenoid cartilages* that sit on the back of the cricoid cartilage. The arytenoid cartilages are smaller than the other two structures, but are very important because they are connected to the vocal cords and are responsible for opening and closing the space in between them.

Back View of Larynx

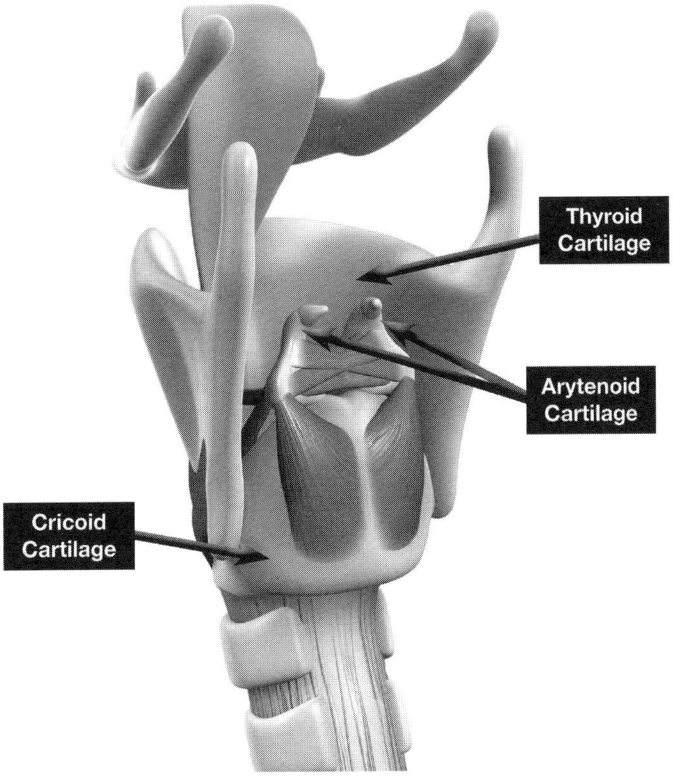

Figure 1.3. Back View of Larynx

The vocal cords are positioned inside this cartilage structure. Attached at one end to the arytenoid cartilages, they run across the space in the center of the larynx over the throat and then attach to the inside of the thyroid cartilage. The vocal cords are not like the strings of a harp or guitar; they are actually two muscles that come together in the middle above the windpipe. The space between the vocal cords is called the *glottis*. The glottis closes and the vocal cords come together when the arytenoid cartilages rotate and squeeze the two muscles toward each other.

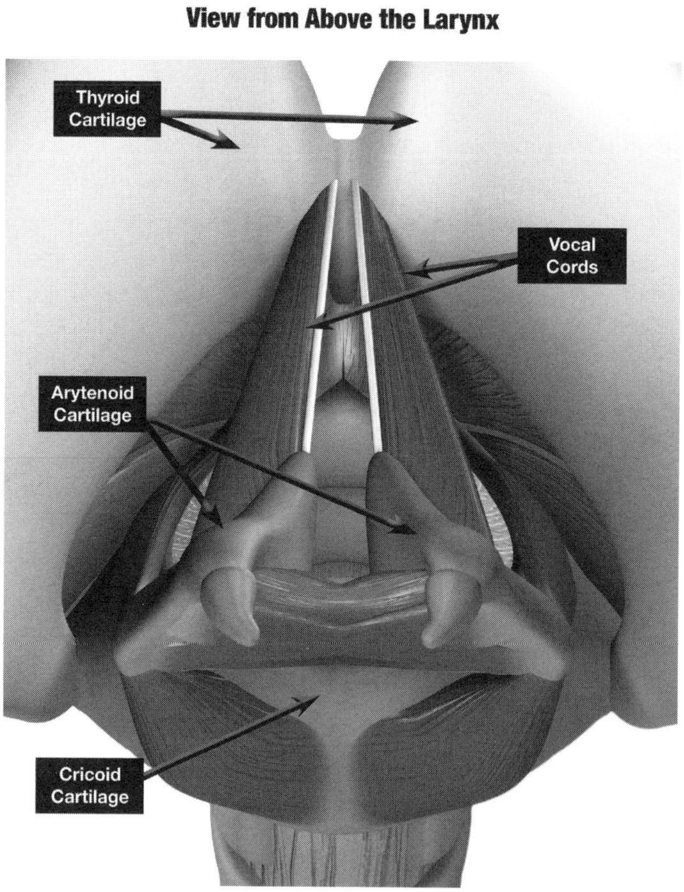

Figure 1.4. Top View of Larynx Including Vocal Cords

For a video tour of the larynx, check out the DVD-ROM:

Video Example 1.1. Tour of the Larynx

Creating Sound

Sound is produced when the glottis is closed and pressure builds up underneath the vocal cords. The pressure is cause by the exhaling of breath from the lungs. Eventually this pressure blasts the vocal cords apart, creating a vibration. With the resulting release in pressure, the vocal cords quickly close again. Then the pressure builds up under the vocal cords again and the process repeats. It's fascinating to note that when a soprano sings a high C, this process is happening inside the larynx over 1,000 times per second! The vibrations created when the cords separate and then come back together are the vibrations that we hear as sound.

The structure of the larynx is responsible for determining the type of vibration that is created by the vocal cords. For example, when we sing higher, the thyroid cartilage rocks forward while the cricoid cartilage rocks back, which stretches out the vocal cords, producing a higher pitch. The opposite takes place as we sing lower. Even different stylistic adjustments are created by the way the vocal cords vibrate. For example, if the arytenoid cartilages are not squeezing the vocal cords together as tightly as they could, extra air escapes between the vocal cords, creating a breathy tone in the voice, like a whisper. There are many more adjustments that these structures within the larynx are capable of making. At this point, it is important that you have a basic understanding of how they work.

Breathing

Breathing plays an important role in the process of creating sound, since it is the energy that causes vocal cord vibration to occur. We'll talk more about breathing and its role in the technique we use in our singing, but first we'll note here that without breath, the larynx is unable to generate sound. It is dependent on the energy originated by breath in order to produce vibrations that we hear as sound.

Resonance

Once the vibration is created, the sound travels through the throat, into the mouth and nasal cavities, through the nose, over the tongue, between the teeth and lips, and finally out into the world. The sound that is first created in the larynx is very different from what we hear once the voice is projected into a room. If you've ever heard someone remove a trumpet's mouthpiece and just blow into it, this is a similar dynamic to what is happening in the larynx. The vibrations expand and gain momentum as they leave the body because of the space that they are traveling through. This is the process of *resonance*. The resonance created by the shape of our throat, mouth, nasal cavity, and tongue are all important factors that determine the characteristics of the sound that we produce.

Summary

Three things are needed to generate the sound of our voice: energy, which is created by the breath; vibration, which takes place in the vocal cords; and resonance, which takes place as the sound travels through the spaces in our head and out into the world.

The Three-Step Process of Creating Sound

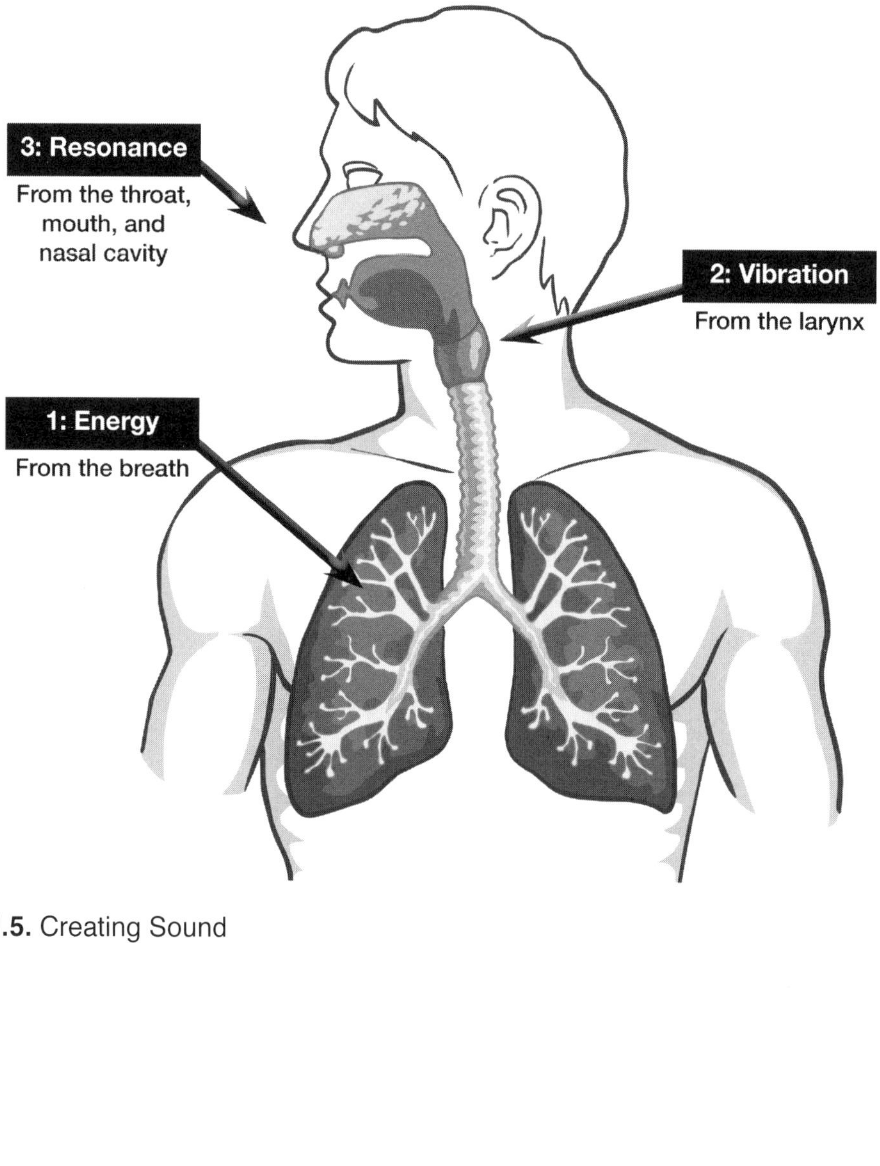

Figure 1.5. Creating Sound

2

Discovering Vocal Freedom

Vocal Freedom

Your ability to increase your range, develop mastery and control of your voice, and protect your voice from damage and misuse lies within the inner workings of the larynx. When you use the instrument without manipulation, freely allowing your voice to function as it is designed to work, you are creating an environment where the voice is performing at its best and the heart can be most fully expressed.

The challenge is that developing the inner workings of the larynx takes time, hard work, and the right game plan to get you where you want to go. It is the athletic aspect of singing. To sing your best you have to develop strength and coordination in the muscles that control all of the aspects of laryngeal function. This book is designed to give you the game plan and tools you need to develop strength and freedom in your voice.

The problem is that most singers have not taken the time to develop the inner workings of the voice in order to perform at the level they are attempting. When the voice is underdeveloped and incapable of the range and versatility that are demanded of it, singers have to rely on quick fixes to help them compensate for the inadequacies of their technique. They rely on muscles outside the larynx to help them sing a little higher, or belt a little louder, navigate that difficult interval, or even simply sing in tune. We refer to any of these manipulations that occur outside of the larynx as *tension*.

The Problem of Vocal Tension

Vocal tension occurs when muscles outside the larynx tighten, twist, pull, and otherwise manipulate the function of the larynx. The first step in developing the potential of the voice is to identify what areas of tension your voice has become reliant on, and, through exercise and retraining muscle memory, eliminate the involvement of those muscles and establish an approach to singing that won't be limited by vocal tension.

Now, singing with tension works—it really does. If you need to sing a little higher than your range is currently developed to sing, you can squeeze your neck muscles or lock your jaw and probably force out some additional range. But what we will see is that every potential area of tension carries limitations. In order to sing at your best, you first have to identify your bad habits and get rid of them. Then you can get to the business of developing a solid foundation of strength and coordination that will unleash the full potential of your voice.

Introduction to Areas of Tension

In this section, I introduce the main areas of vocal tension. As I describe their characteristics, limitations, and effects on the voice, identify the areas of tension that are holding back your potential. You may find that you can relate to every one of them—and if that's the case, congratulations; you'll have plenty to work on during your practice sessions! Most likely there will be two to three that really stand out as having your name written all over them. You'll recognize the characteristics and you'll relate to their effects and limitations on your voice. Take note of which areas of tension you feel are currently a part of your technique. Once you've identified your tension areas, there will be practical tips and exercises to help you eliminate that tension and discover freedom for your voice. This will be the first step in developing your own personal workout plan.

Neck Tension

The neck is probably the most common area of tension for singers. We've all seen it. The singer is going for the big high note at the end of the song and the head tilts up, the chin thrusts forward, and all the veins start popping out of the neck. The singer looks like he or she is trying to squeeze out one last pull-up over the bar.

Like all areas of tension, neck tension serves a purpose. It helps you sing a little higher (especially in your chest voice), and it can help you sing a little louder. But, like every other area of tension, neck tension limits your vocal potential and has some poor effects on the quality of your sound.

Singers who sing with neck tension often have a "shouty" or "yelly" quality that's accentuated the higher they go. To help them go higher in their range, they are involving the *sternocleidomastoid* muscles that connect from the sternum to just behind the ears. These muscles run alongside the larynx, and when they squeeze the sides of the larynx the restriction helps the vocal cords produce higher pitches. The problem is that it also constricts the space in the back of the throat, so the higher you go, the smaller the space you have to sing with. Once you get toward the top of your range, you may be able to strain out a couple of extra notes, but you also have to force those notes through this tiny space—hence the "shouty" or "yelly" quality as you try to squeeze a big tone through a small hole.

Our voice requires freedom and space, especially in the upper range and at high volumes. We need the neck muscles to remain completely relaxed, regardless of how high or loudly we are singing. This will allow the throat to stay relaxed and open, allowing for natural resonance and great tone throughout your range. It will also extend your range. If you are using neck tension to sing higher, the higher you go, the more tension you have to engage. Eventually you will hit a point where the throat closes and the voice, which can no longer sustain the strain, will squeeze off. By relaxing the neck muscles and allowing the throat to remain open, you will be able to sing higher than you would if you were using neck tension.

A great way to eliminate neck tension is to sing a five-note ascending scale on "ah." At the end of each scale, modulate up by one half step.

Figure 2.1. Neck Tension Exercise

Audio Example 2.1. Neck Tension Exercise

As you sing, simply roll your head from side to side, and forward and back. As you do this, you may find that your neck wants to reach up and out, especially as you increase pitch and volume. Relax your neck muscles, and watch in the mirror to make sure there is no reach. It may feel strange and you may have a sense that your voice will crack, or that there is no stability as you sing. This is natural, as you are retraining your coordination. As the inner workings of the larynx are strengthened through repetition and conditioning—and as neck tension is reduced more and more—you will gradually find greater strength and stability than you've ever had. Be patient with the process, and do not rely on old technique (tension) to give you a greater sense of security. This will only reinforce bad habits and slow down the process.

Jaw Tension

Jaw tension requires a little bit more explanation in order to show how something so far away from the larynx can cause problems for our singing. Neck tension makes sense. The sternocleidomastoid muscles run right along the sides of the larynx, and when they tighten, they squeeze the larynx. But with jaw tension, what we're monitoring is the hinge of the jaw, just below and in front of the ears. How much does what's happening all the way up there really have to do with what's happening with the larynx?

Let's try this little experiment. Take your pointer fingers and find the hinge of your jaw. Open your mouth and close it, and you should feel that joint adjusting as you do. Keep your pointer fingers there. Now take your thumbs and find the front of your larynx. It's the little bump on the front of your throat. We'll describe how to identify it in more detail when we discuss laryngeal tension, but for now as long as you are in the general area it will be good enough. Once you have your pointer fingers on your jaw and your thumbs on (or near) your larynx, thrust your jaw forward (like you have a really bad underbite) and clench it. Now swallow and feel what is happening down in your throat by your larynx. Don't swallow too hard, or you might sprain something! Most likely you felt a lot of resistance in your throat as you tried to swallow, and quite possibly you couldn't even swallow at all.

The muscles that we use to swallow are located around the larynx, and they actually assist in moving the larynx up and down as we swallow. If tightening the jaw makes it difficult to swallow, and in some cases immobilizes the muscles we use to swallow, we can see that there is a very strong correlation between what's happening with the jaw and what's happening in the throat.

Jaw tension makes it very difficult for the voice to adjust and maneuver to the places it needs to go. You see, we play a very fluid and organic instrument. The voice is not a static instrument with keys and levers; it is a constantly changing, living organism that needs to be free to shift and adjust through the process of singing. Every pitch we sing requires the voice to take on a slightly different form. Every stylistic nuance we bring into our voice requires an adjustment. Changes in volume, register, and tone all require the voice to shift. Jaw tension bogs down the voice and makes these adjustments difficult, if not impossible. It's a bit like dumping a bucket of molasses into the transmission of your car; you're going to have some challenges when it's time to change gears. A car needs to shift gears as the demands you place on it as a driver change.

I learned to drive in a 1974 Volkswagen Bus. It was two shades of neon green—a lighter green on the top and a darker green on the bottom, separated by neon blue stripes in the middle. It was a manual transmission with a stick shift that was about three feet long. Now, when you're sixteen years old and driving around your small town in the Sweet Pickles bus, and you don't want to do that shimmy through the intersection as the car judders between stalling and taking off, first gear is a very good thing! However, first gear at 60 miles an hour down the freeway—not so much! And yet as singers we do this to ourselves all the time. We engage jaw tension at some point as we are singing, and then our voice locks and we try to take that same coordination through other areas of vocal production. This is not how the voice is designed to work. We need the voice to be fluid and flexible, and to adjust as we change pitch, modify dynamics, or bring stylistic colors to our tone.

Many of the challenges that singers face can be traced to jaw tension. When I begin working with someone who is experiencing problems transitioning between chest voice and head voice, often the first thing I will do is to try to alleviate jaw tension. Pitch problems, too, can be the result of jaw tension, since the resistance that makes it difficult for the voice to shift and maneuver naturally impedes control and accuracy.

The jaw needs to be relaxed and free—completely uninvolved in vocal production. Massaging the jaw as you sing different exercises and songs is a great way to eliminate tension and allow the jaw to relax. Try singing this exercise alternating between "ah" and "ee," using only your tongue to change between the vowels. The jaw should not move at all. Allow the jaw to simply hang loose as if it is disconnected from the rest of your head. If you drool on yourself while you sing this exercise, you get extra credit!

Figure 2.2. Jaw Tension Exercise

Audio Example 2.2. Jaw Tension Exercise

Laryngeal Tension

Another common form of tension, especially for modern (nonoperatic) styles, is laryngeal tension. If the larynx rises up in the throat, the tone will get thin and whiny, losing depth and warmth, especially in the higher range.

Have you ever heard recordings of yourself and felt like the upper pitches were pinched off? If you want to get more fullness and depth (guts!) to your upper range, you've got to exercise the coordination and muscles that anchor the larynx down so that it doesn't rise up in the throat. So how do you do that? What does it feel like to lower the larynx and drop it in your throat? Here's how you do it.

Find your larynx again. Remember, it's the bump on the front of your throat. Guys, we call this your Adam's apple, and most of you won't have any problem finding it at all. Ladies, it's a little trickier for you because your larynx is a fraction of the size of the male larynx. The way you find it is to slide your finger down the front of your throat. As you do you will feel a bump with a notch in the front that forms a V shape. That's the thyroid cartilage—the front of your larynx.

Once you've found it, place all four fingers around it, positioning two above it and two below it, so that if it moves you won't lose it. Now yawn and notice how your larynx drops down in your throat. Notice how your throat feels like it is expanding inside and everything feels wide and open. This is the coordination you are looking for.

Sing the five-note scale on an "oo." As you do, monitor the position of the larynx and yawn the throat as open as possible to keep it down. After each scale, modulate up by one half step.

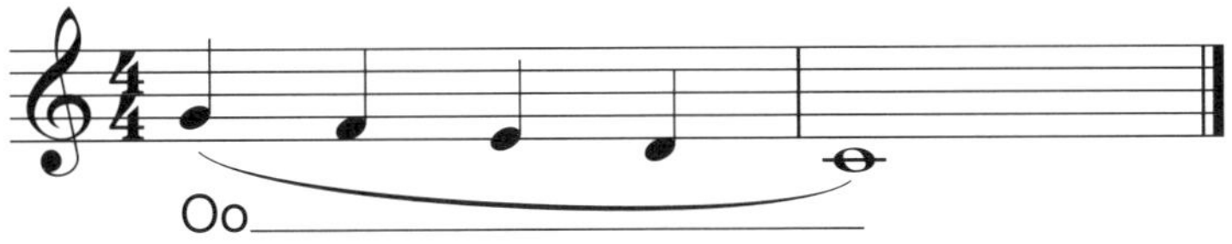

Figure 2.3. Laryngeal Tension Exercise

Audio Example 2.3. Laryngeal Tension Exercise

Does your larynx rise up as you go higher in your range? If it does, add laryngeal tension to the list—this will need to be part of your development plan. As you continue higher, the amount of yawn that you feel in your throat will need to increase. The higher you go, the more you need to yawn your throat open.

It is important to note that the tone that you produce when the larynx is down is a fuller, more classical-sounding tone. A truly descended larynx is associated with an operatic sound. This is okay. Even if you have no intention of singing in a classical style, this will be good for you and will not get in the way of any other style that you want to sing in.

Vocalize Classically

I am a vocal coach for modern styles (pop, jazz, rock, etc.). A lot of my clients get nervous when we start working together and I have them going through their vocal workout singing in a classical style. They've watched *American Idol*; they know that when the judges say a singer sounds "trained," they mean that's not what they want to hear. But vocalizing with a classical tone doesn't mean you'll be stuck singing your songs with a classical tone. What it will do is provide an environment where certain aspects of your voice will expand and strengthen in a way that singing modern styles simply won't ever develop.

Controlling the larynx is one of the benefits you will receive from vocalizing with a classical tone. Modern styles actually require a slightly raised larynx in order to sound authentic to the style. Because of this, if you only sing in a modern style, the muscles that anchor the larynx down will never get a workout and your larynx will rise up too high in the throat and cause you problems. The only way to work on this coordination is to sing classically when you are vocalizing. Over time, and with consistent practice, the position of the larynx will become a conscious choice, a coordination that you can voluntarily control. Working in this way will strengthen the muscles and solidify the coordination into your muscle memory so that when you go to sing in a modern style, you can add just enough of that feeling of expanse in the back of your throat to keep the larynx down, extend your range, and improve your tone.

I caution young singers who want to make a career in modern styles against pursuing a classical performance degree in a college or university setting. Developing the descended-larynx tone is an important supplement to the singing you do in modern styles. However, if the focus of your singing for four years in a classical music institution is a full, dropped-larynx sound, and you rarely (if ever) sing with any other tone, you will be very challenged to develop the ability to produce a sound that will be marketable in modern styles. It can be done; I've worked with some folks who came to me completely locked in a classical vocal production and tone who now sing with as much stylistic flair as anyone in the industry, but it took a lot of hard work to pull them out of those ruts. There is a big difference between using this as a supplemental technique, and having it as a steady diet over a number of years.

Lip, Face, and Cheek Tension

Identifying lip, face, and cheek tension is best done by watching for them in a mirror. What you're watching for is anything you do that looks weird. If a high note looks like you're hurt, there's tension in your face that is going to affect your voice. What you want to see is a relaxed, energized, and natural-looking you!

Use a Mirror

The mirror is critical for eliminating most areas of tension. As long as you actually look into it and use it, you will recognize tension areas that would have gone unnoticed otherwise, and often simply seeing them show up in the mirror is enough to allow you to identify the tension and make the adjustment to relax those muscles. Many singers have been singing with tension for decades. The thing that feels natural is to tighten those muscles as you sing. Don't fool yourself into thinking that you'll feel tension when it creeps in—you won't. You've been doing it for so long that it feels "right." Most tension areas will need visual reinforcement to be identified, and lip, face, and cheek tension is certainly no exception.

A great exercise for relieving lip, face, and cheek tension is the lip-buzz exercise. To do this, keep your lips together and spit while you sing. It's a very loose, relaxed production that is a lot like what a kid would do to blow bubbles in a pool of water. Keep the vibration going through the phrase and simply allow the voice to adjust however it does naturally as you "sing" the exercise.

Figure 2.4. Lip, Face, and Cheek Tension Exercise

Audio Example 2.4. Lip, Face, and Cheek Tension Exercise

Tongue Tension

The tongue is probably the most universal area of tension that needs attention in the clients I have worked with—everybody struggles with it. It's also the area of tension that gets the least amount of press—no one talks about it! I had never even heard of tongue tension until I went to graduate school. And it's the hardest area of tension to detect. The reason for the elusiveness of tongue tension is that it is completely an internal tension, with very little external evidence for us to monitor.

The tongue is a large, complex combination of muscles that extends down the back of the throat. We often think of the tongue as only what we can see in our mouth, but the majority of the tongue is hidden from us. As the tongue goes back in the throat it gets larger and connects at the base to the hyoid bone, located just above the thyroid cartilage in the larynx. The area of the tongue that causes us problems is this back part attached to the hyoid bone. If the tongue pulls back while we are singing, the hyoid bone will press against the larynx, causing tension for the voice and closing off space in the back of the throat, much as laryngeal tension does as the larynx rises up.

So how do we keep this back part of the tongue from retreating and causing us problems when we can't even see it when it's happening? Well, there is a technique to correct this, although it's not a very popular one with anyone I've ever worked with. What you do is take a Handi Wipe cloth (you can buy these at any Target or Walmart and at most grocery stores), cut it up into 1" x 4" strips, and use a strip to grab ahold of the tongue, pulling it out of your mouth as far as you can, stopping just before the point of pain! With your tongue hanging out of your mouth, and your hand firmly gripping it, begin to sing a song or exercise on a wide-open "ah" vowel. Make sure that you sing "ah" as in father and not "a" as in apple.

Figure 2.5. Tongue Tension Exercise

Audio Example 2.5. Tongue Tension Exercise

As you sing through the exercise, you may notice the tongue pulling back. Don't worry. No matter how severe a case of tongue tension someone has had, I've never seen anyone's tongue pull that arm back down the throat! If you feel resistance, expand the throat like a yawn, arch the tongue forward, and create as much space as possible in the throat. With time and repetition over weeks and months, you should feel the tongue gradually relax and develop to the point where you can sing through your entire range with the tongue hanging, unmoving, out of your mouth.

Vocal Damage and Tension

In addition to the benefits that alleviating tension will have on your overall tone, control, and vocal range, you will also be protecting your voice from fatigue and damage.

Singing with tension is exhausting on your voice. Since tension introduces an outside force and strain on the voice, it alters the way the vocal cords vibrate and the way they come together to produce sound. Now, that may not seem like that big of a deal, but consider that when a soprano is singing a high C her vocal cords are coming apart and back together again over 1,000 times per second (yes, you read that correctly—per second!). With that amount of consistent contact, any manipulation that throws off that coordination can have some serious effects on the health of our voice. Interrupting the natural coordination of that vibration will cause the cords to come together either awkwardly or with strain. This can irritate the vocal cords and cause them to swell. Swelling of the vocal cords (or laryngitis) causes the voice to become hoarse, limiting your range and vocal ability and shortening the amount of time you can sing. If you find yourself losing your voice at the end of a two-hour rehearsal or by the end of a long day of services, freeing your voice from tension is the first step in increasing your endurance.

If the misuse of your voice becomes chronic, and tension is ingrained into your vocal production, you are at risk of damaging your voice, even to the point of a permanent injury. What happens here is that after the cords become inflamed to protect themselves, the next layer of defense against an irritation on the vocal cord is a polyp (very similar to a blister). Now remember, the vocal cords are coming apart and back together again hundreds of times per second. If they are smacking together abrasively or awkwardly because of tension, the body will protect that point of impact and sensitivity with a polyp, just as our feet do when our new pair of shoes is rubbing and irritating a particular spot. As long as we stop the irritation and allow the body to repair, the body will absorb the polyp and the lining of the vocal cord will repair itself, just as our foot can absorb a blister. However, if the irritation continues, the polyp will turn to a hard nodule (very similar to a callus on our feet), which is permanent and requires surgical removal.

How do you know if you have a polyp or nodule? Usually a polyp or nodule is accompanied by chronic hoarseness and a raspy sound to the voice. Often there are also pitches toward the middle of the range that will no longer phonate, even if the singer can still vocalize above and below them. If you suspect you may have a polyp or nodule, the only way to know for certain is to be examined by an otolaryngologist to rule out any possibility of vocal damage.

The best defense against misuse, fatigue, and damage is to first eliminate tension from your voice, and then further develop your voice using the techniques presented in the rest of this book. Almost all vocal problems can be corrected with these adjustments to your technique.

3

Breathing and Support

Breathing: Energy for Singing

Once a singer has identified the areas of tension holding back his or her success, it is important not only to eliminate those tension areas, but to also replace the energy initially provided by the tension with something else. But where do we get energy for singing?

Energy for singing comes from proper breath support. Most singers have heard that breathing is important for singing and that there is a right way to do it. It's hard to spend any amount of time singing in a choir or pursuing vocal training without receiving some instruction on breathing technique. But many of the singers I've worked with, even some who have pursued degrees in vocal performance, are unsure of the best way to use breath and support to energize the voice. It is essential to our vocal health and growth to understand this technique and to confidently and consistently use it in our singing. So how does it work?

First, let's take a look at how not to breathe.

High Breathing

Many singers begin their pursuit of singing with this type of breathing coordination. High breathing is a breath that is focused in the upper chest. It usually involves a heaving of the chest and a lift in the shoulders and is often very audible, projecting a loud gasp when the singer breathes in. This kind of breathing actually causes tension in the voice as the chest, neck, and shoulders lift up. The amount of breath we gain using this coordination is minimal and insufficient, as much of the breath we take in is being forced and restricted into the upper chest cavity. You can see if this is the type of breathing you use when you sing by simply watching in the mirror, or by placing a hand on your upper chest near your collarbone and taking a deep breath in, watching to see if there is any lift to the chest or shoulders. If you see or feel any movement at all in the upper chest or shoulders, then it's time to get to work on a new technique for breathing.

Developing a New Technique for Breathing

Low breathing is a technique for breathing that uses the diaphragm and the intercostal muscles between our ribs to create space for the lungs to fully expand with air. Here's how it works. As we breathe in, the intercostals lift the rib cage and expand it outward to the sides. At the same time the diaphragm, a large, dome-shaped muscle that sits under the lungs, flexes and flattens out, creating space under the lungs as it pushes against the viscera (fancy term for "guts"). It's accurate to think of the diaphragm as the bulldozer muscle, since it serves to push the soft, squishy, moveable stuff of the viscera (large and small intestines, liver, kidneys) out of the way.

As the diaphragm does its work creating space under the lungs, the abdominal muscles must relax and expand out. If the singer's gut doesn't expand out, this breathing technique doesn't work! If the abdomen stays tight and pulled in, there is nowhere for the viscera to go, and the diaphragm will be unable to create enough space for the lungs to fully expand. This is often the most difficult aspect of this breathing technique, because most singers don't want to stick their gut out, especially on a stage with hundreds or even thousands of eyeballs watching them. Get over it! You'll be the one who notices the most, and unless you're wearing spandex while you lead worship (which I wouldn't recommend for a variety of reasons) the expansion will go unnoticed by anyone in attendance.

For a video demonstrating this breathing technique, check out the DVD-ROM:

Video Example 3.1. Breathing Technique

Here are a couple of exercises that will help you begin to work on this coordination for breathing:

Breathing Exercise 1

Lie down on the ground, on your back. Place one of your hands against your belly button and press down slightly. The other hand should be resting on your upper chest, by your collarbone. With your hands in place, push all of the air out, making sure that you feel your stomach drop down toward the floor. Then, over eight counts, slowly breathe in, allowing the abdomen to relax and rise up as you expand the lungs for a full breath. It is important that you only feel movement in the abdomen, and that the upper chest remain completely still and motionless.

Then, over the next eight counts, breathe out, feeling the abdomen drop back down toward the floor. Continue this process, making sure that all of the coordination and movement is happening only in the abdomen with no involvement at all in the upper chest. Once you feel like you're getting great consistency on the floor, try standing up and see if you can achieve the same consistency there as well.

Breathing Exercise 2

Begin this exercise again lying flat on the ground, continuing to monitor the abdomen with one hand and the upper chest with the other. This time the breath in will happen faster, and rather than simply breathing out, sing a five-note scale, modulating by half steps after each scale is completed.

Figure 3.1. Breathing Exercise 2

Audio Example 3.1. Breathing Exercise

Just as in Breathing Exercise 1, once you feel you're getting great consistency on the floor, try standing up and see if you can achieve the same consistency there as well.

Should I Breathe Through My Nose or Through My Mouth?

Breathing through your nose provides some nice benefits in that it warms the air by the time it reaches your throat, and doesn't dry your throat out as much as inhaling through your mouth. However, when you inhale through your nose it takes around three to five seconds to completely fill the lungs. Rarely, if ever, do we have that much time available to us in the middle of a song—the band isn't going to vamp for an extra measure while we take a breath! So it's best to practice breathing through your mouth, since that's what you're going to need to do in performance.

What I've described so far is the process of breathing, which involves acquiring as much air as possible and "filling the tank." This is critical, but the most important part of the process is what I refer to as support, which involves translating the air we get when we breathe into energy for our singing. Here's how this works.

Support

Let's quickly review the process of inhalation. The rib cage expands, the diaphragm pushes down, and the abdomen goes out, right? Now we're ready to allow that air out and sing. What we do not want to do is to simply allow the air to run out as if we were a balloon with a giant leak. We need to efficiently use the breath we have to provide energy and support for our singing. How do we do that?

The key component in support is the strength and coordination of the diaphragm. Once the diaphragm has flexed and forced the viscera down and out, creating space for the lungs to expand, we want it to remain engaged as we exhale and sing out, pushing down and out against the involuntary tightening of the abdominal muscles. See figure 3.2.

What does that feel like? For those of you ladies who have experienced childbirth (on the giving end—we've all been on the receiving end), the internal muscles you used to push life out into the world, that's exactly the pushing-down coordination we are looking for. For the rest of us, our reference point will be the feeling of engaging our, eh, um, bathroom muscles: an internal bearing down as we are singing out (a gentle one, don't get carried away

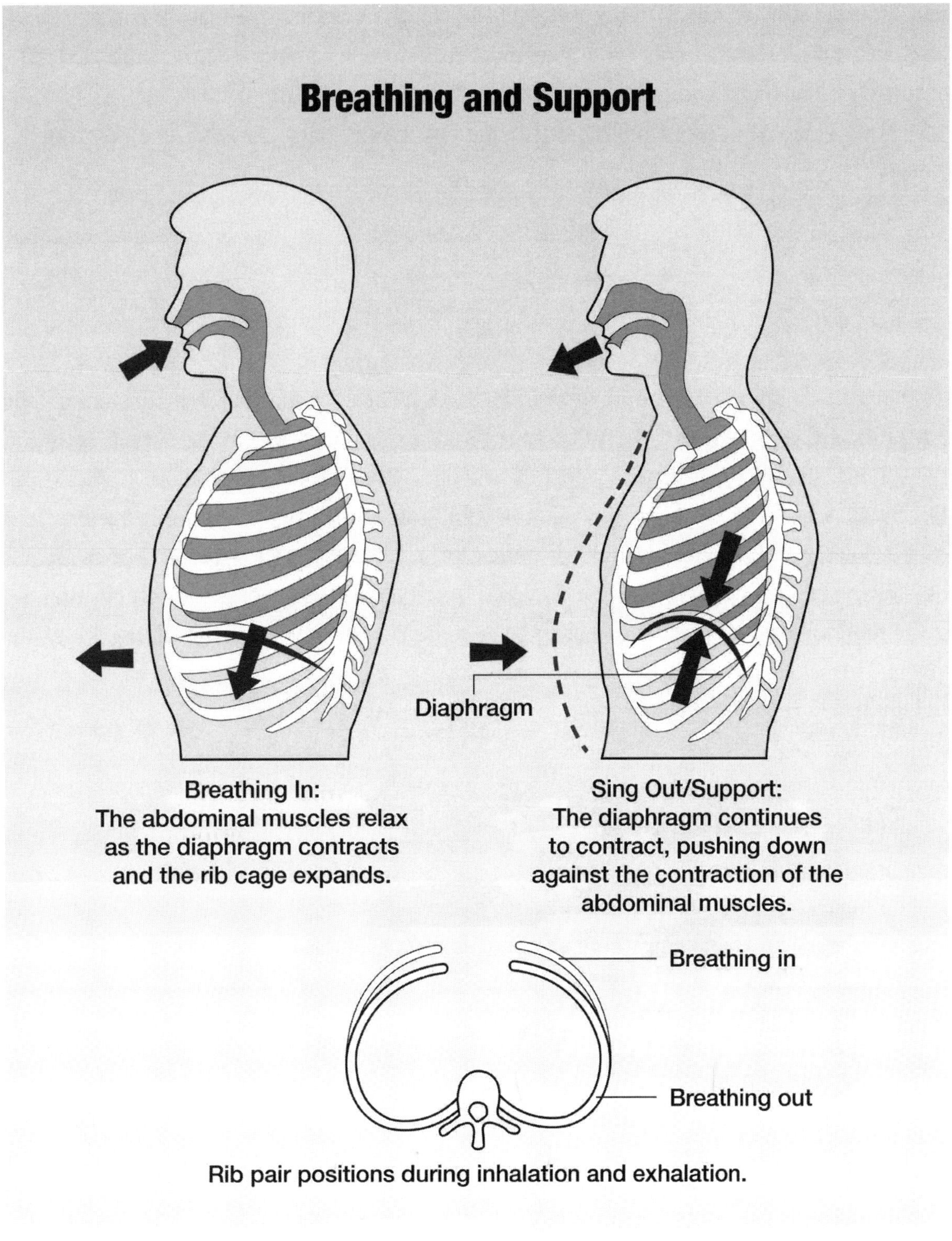

Figure 3.2. Breathing Diagram

with it, especially on stage!). That feeling will keep the diaphragm engaged, pushing down and out against the constriction of the abdominal muscles as the breath is released. The antagonism between those muscles is what provides energy for the voice.

For a video demonstrating this technique for support, check out the DVD-ROM:

Video Example 3.2. Support Demonstration

Support Exercise 1

Try this. Lie down on the ground, on your back. Place both of your hands against your belly button and press down slightly. With your hands pressing down, take a deep breath and then shout out, "Hey!" Make it a deep, full, and open shout, not a tight yell or a high scream. Deep and full! Notice that as you do this your stomach presses up and out against your hand's downward pressure. If you didn't notice it the first time, try it again and be conscious of allowing your stomach to press out as you shout. The feeling of your stomach pushing out is the diaphragm pressing down in order to energize the shout you are generating with your voice. This is the feeling (that internal push down) that you need to engage as you sing in order to provide energy for your voice and to allow tension to relax.

Support Exercise 2

On this exercise, breathe in deeply, and as you exhale bring your teeth together and hiss like a snake. As the air is slowly escaping on this "Tssssss" sound, push down and out in your abdomen. This is a great exercise to really *feel* the coordination of internal diaphragmatic support.

Audio Example 3.2. Support Exercise

4

Increasing Vocal Range

The Registers

Everyone wants to increase his or her vocal range. It is probably the number one request I receive when I begin working with someone. But how do we do it? Many factors contribute to our ability to increase our range, and some of them we've already covered. Vocal tension can greatly inhibit our range. Proper breath support can provide energy for our voice that will help us expand our range. But the most important aspect of increasing our range involves the development of the *registers* of the voice.

"Register" is an official term we use to describe two very different physiological functions within the voice. Most often, though, we refer to these different functions as *head voice* (or falsetto) and *chest voice* (or belt voice).

I don't know if you've ever thought of it this way, but you essentially have two instruments in one. Every singer uses two main physiological processes that affect the shape and function of the vocal cords and ultimately create two very different sounds. Each register has a different set of muscles that are responsible for making the adjustments that determine what pitches we are singing, and the type of tone we produce. Head voice requires a very unique muscular coordination when we sing. The muscles that become engaged are very different from those involved in chest voice, as is the effect that this coordination has on the vocal cords, their shape, the way they vibrate, and the tone they produce. The same is true for chest voice. It's like having a trumpet and a clarinet all wrapped up into the same instrument.

To sing with our full range, we need to understand each of these unique registers, and to develop the full strength and ability of both head voice and chest voice. The stronger the muscles are in both registers, and the more we solidify the coordination of each, the greater our range will become.

The Beginning

We first began using the terms "head voice" and "chest voice" back in the 1600s. The terms originated with the *bel canto* teachers in Italy who came onto the scene after the birth of opera. For the first time in history music was being written that required great vocal ability to sing, and the people who could do it were the superstars of that era. Everyone wanted to become the next "Italian Idol," and so for the first time in history people were interested in learning how to train and develop the voice. With the birth of opera came the birth of the vocal coach.

These first vocal coaches were more limited than we are today in their knowledge of the human body and the way it functions. The Catholic Church at that time forbade the dissection of corpses, and so theories of the structure of the human body and the way it functions were all formulated without any awareness of what was really under our skin.

The teachers of that time believed that there was a long hallway or *passaggio* running up the back of our chest, neck, and head like an elevator shaft, which the voice traveled up and down like an elevator car. At the top of the vocal range, they believed the voice was actually up in the head, so they called this the *voce di testa*, or head voice. At the bottom of the vocal range, they believed that the voice was actually down in the chest, so they called that the *voce di petto*, or chest voice.

We now know that all of our vocal sound is produced by the vocal cords, located inside the larynx, and that the voice "stays" in our throat as long as we are singing. What the old Italians were describing was the sensation that singers generally feel when they sing in the two registers. So don't get too hung up on the terms: the sensation of singing in head voice or chest voice varies greatly from person to person. Below we'll look in more detail at the true characteristics of these registers, and how we can develop them in order to realize the full potential of our vocal range.

Characteristics of Head Voice

Physiology

When we sing in head voice, the cricoid cartilage at the base of the larynx rocks backward, and the thyroid cartilage rocks forward. This movement stretches the vocal cords and they become long and thin. This stretching affects the vibration of the vocal cords, so that only the innermost part of the larynx, right next to the opening between the vocal cords (the glottis), is vibrating.

Tone

This vibration, "lighter" than the vibration in chest voice, produces a corresponding change in tone. The tone produced by the head voice is often described as light, airy, "floaty," ethereal, sweet, and pretty. It also affects the way a singer experiences the head-voice production. When you sing in head voice there is little amplitude of sound. In other words, the vibration isn't causing too much racket in your throat or the rest of your head. Much of the vibration is being projected out into the room, and a great deal of what you hear of your head voice is what is actually bouncing around the room and coming into your ear. This is very different from the way we experience chest voice, which we'll examine below. Be sure to read that discussion to further understand how differently a singer experiences chest voice and head voice.

Range

When the vocal cords are stretched as they are in head voice, they can extend to higher pitches, which is why the head voice will always allow you to sing higher than you can sing in the chest voice register.

However, the head voice can also be carried down throughout your entire range. You can sing in head voice as low as you can in chest voice, and you actually want to work toward this, with the aim of building as much crossover as possible between the registers. The head voice has the potential for a great deal of volume and fullness in the middle to upper part of the range, but as you carry the head voice down, the tone will get lighter and breathier. This is because the cords remain stretched in the head-voice production. In the lower range, the only way to eliminate this breathiness and fill out the tone is to blend in chest voice. The pure head voice will always be light and breathy at the bottom of the range.

Characteristics of Chest Voice

Physiology

When we sing in chest voice, the cricoid cartilage at the base of the larynx rocks forward, and the thyroid cartilage rocks backward. This movement shortens the vocal cords and they become thick. This shortening and thickening affects the vibration of the vocal cords: in chest voice, the entire vocal cord vibrates, with ripples that run throughout the muscle of the vocal cord.

Tone

The tone that we create when we sing in chest voice is often described as full, strong, loud, meaty, gutsy, and powerful. This aggressive vibration creates all kinds of racket as the amplitude of sound is increased. The vibration of the sound waves coming off of the vocal cords in chest voice causes sympathetic vibration in the throat and even the bone structure of the head. These vibrations travel into the inner ear, so much of what the singer experiences in chest voice is not what is bouncing around the room for others to hear, but rather internal vibrations.

This creates some unique challenges for the singer in the development process. Singers who sing primarily in their chest voice are addicted to power. They are familiar with the volume, intensity, and buzz that are created when they sing in chest voice, and they love it! When chest-voice singers transition to head voice (sometimes by accident and often because it's their only alternative when the range gets high) they feel as if the bottom has just dropped out of their voice. They feel like they have no substance and power in the head voice, and that their transition into that register comes across as a total cop-out. This is not necessarily true about how the voice is being heard by others in the room, but it is certainly true for how the singer experiences the sound.

Singers who usually sing in head voice are used to hearing their voice with much less amplitude of sound. Much of what they are used to hearing is the sound that bounces around the room and enters their ear externally—just the way it does for the listener. When head-voice singers begin using the chest voice, they are horrified at the brash, unbridled, and over-the-top sound they hear themselves making. They are hearing (sometimes for the first time) a great deal of internal vibration accompanying their singing, and they don't like it! I've even had clients who physically jumped because they scared themselves the first time they managed to sing in chest voice.

We will talk more about how to develop the registers and how to work with these dynamics, but it is important to be aware of these characteristics unique to each register as we get started.

Range

The chest voice, no matter how developed it is, how free you are from tension, or how good your breath support has become, will never allow you to sing as high as the head voice. There will always be notes above the chest voice that you will only be able to sing with your head voice. This is because of the shortness and thickness of the cords in this production. As you extend your range in the chest voice, the cords also stretch, and a tug-of-war begins to take place between the muscles. You are trying to hold the production in chest voice, but the muscles responsible for head voice are becoming more and more active and are very eager to take over. Often, at the top of the chest voice range, this transition into head voice will take place without the singer's intention, and the head voice will "pop" into gear. This abrupt change creates a "crack" or "flip" in the voice. While it is often avoided in performance, this abrupt transition is a powerful way for us to distinguish between the head voice and chest voice and will be an important aspect of the first step in developing the registers.

A Three-Step Process

Developing the full range of your voice is a three-step process, and we will thoroughly explore the details of each step.

Here are the three steps:

1. Isolating the Registers
2. Building Overlap
3. Blending the Registers

Step 1: Isolating the Registers

The first step in the process of developing the registers is to isolate the registers. Many singing techniques focus initially on smoothing out the break and coordinating the registers. This is a great goal, but you can't hope to smoothly transition from one register to the next if one or both of the registers is weak at the transition point. You also can't coordinate and blend two things together if you don't have two things to start with. Many singers are frustrated because they can't successfully blend or mix the voice, without realizing that this coordination requires a developed chest voice and a developed head voice.

So we begin by separating the registers, working independently on each one before we move on to coordinating and blending.

The Yodel Flip

Many singers aren't aware of when they are in head voice and when they are in chest voice. Some can't tell the difference between the two productions at all, and some are unsure in certain parts of their range.

A great way to help define the difference between head voice and chest voice, and to know for certain which register you are using at any given time, is to use the yodel or crack in the voice. When a singer goes immediately from head voice to chest voice, or vice versa, the voice will automatically flip or crack as a by-product of this fast, uncoordinated transition.

Your voice will not crack if you transition from one note to the next and remain in the same register; it only happens when you change registers. If you are singing an exercise in chest voice and then you jump up to a note in your head voice, and your voice cracks, then you know that everything before the crack was chest voice, and the production immediately following it was head voice. The yodel makes very clear to the singer the difference between these register adjustments.

The easiest interval for finding the yodel is an octave. Simply sustain a note in a pure isolated head voice (very light and floaty), and then immediately drop down a full octave to a full isolated chest voice (very strong and forceful). The goal is for the voice to crack when you do. It's going to sound bad when you first start doing it. Not only will you hear this awful, donkey-sounding crack, but, because of the quick adjustment between registers, the pitch accuracy may not be what you are used to. It's okay; the pitch accuracy will improve, but the crack will always remain for this exercise—get used to it. If you ever do the exercise and it sounds smooth and coordinated, that's nice, but you're doing the exercise completely wrong. It's all about getting an obnoxious and ugly crack in your voice between the registers.

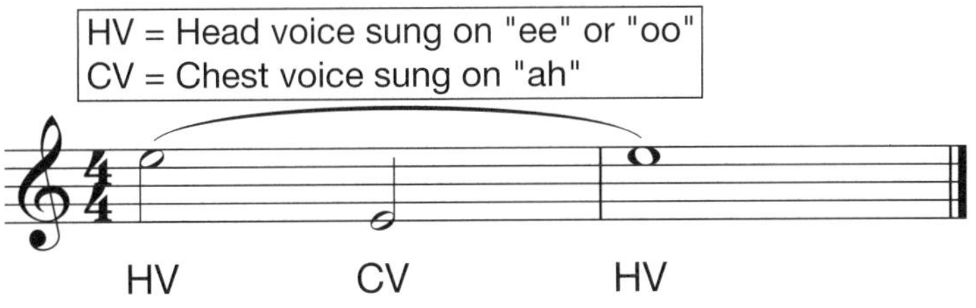

Figure 4.1. Octave Yodel Exercise 1

Audio Example 4.1. Octave Yodel Exercise 1

Some singers have a hard time beginning with the octave yodel going from high to low. That's okay; if it's easier to get your voice to crack going from chest to head, try to achieve the octave yodel going from low to high. You may also try transitioning quickly between the registers, as fast as you can, to help find the crack in your voice. You can find an example of this on the accompanying CD.

Figure 4.2. Octave Yodel Exercise 2

Audio Example 4.2. Octave Yodel Exercise 2

Once the coordination of the yodel is established on an octave, begin shortening the interval of the notes that you are cracking between. A great next-step exercise to develop your chest voice begins with a five-note scale that cracks up to head voice as illustrated below:

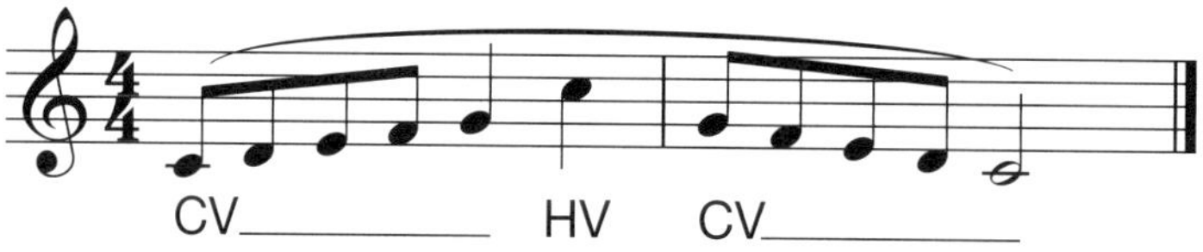

Figure 4.3. Ascending Chest Voice Yodel Exercise

Be sure to stay in a very full isolated chest voice all the way to the fifth note, then immediately transition to a light isolated head voice as you flip up to the sixth note of the exercise, and then immediately back to the chest voice on the next pitch and through the remainder of the exercise. If you begin to soften the chest voice as you go up the scale, you won't get a yodel flip. Maintain a very aggressive approach in the chest voice all the way up to the point when you abruptly change to head voice, and then do the same on the way back down. Carry this exercise up and down throughout your range, modulating by half steps to the very highest notes you can sing in chest voice, then down to the very lowest notes you can sing.

Another, similar exercise can help you isolate the registers and develop the head voice. Begin in the head voice and come down a five-note scale in a very pure and light isolated head voice. Then immediately transition to a full isolated chest voice, and then immediately back to head voice on the next note and throughout the rest of the exercise, as indicated on the staff below. Again, the goal is the yodel. If you transition smoothly and it sounds beautiful, the exercise is a total failure. If the crack between the registers is horrific and has the neighbors wondering if you are housing farm animals in your guest room, you are doing it exactly right!

Figure 4.4. Descending Head Voice Yodel Exercise

Once you have mastered these exercises, try graduating to the following exercises, yodeling on each transition between the registers.

Figure 4.5. Ascending Major Scale Yodel Exercise

Figure 4.6. Descending Major Scale Yodel Exercise

Establishing the coordination of the yodel is critical before working to develop the registers. Too often I have come across a singer who thought she was developing her chest voice, only to find out that she was only singing in a very loud and forced head voice. The yodel defines the difference between the registers. The distinction that is important to establish for yourself is the difference in the feeling, not the sound. Do not trust your ears, because you will sound different in every environment in which you sing. Trust the feeling and coordination that takes place in your throat when you yodel. A true yodel click will almost feel like your larynx just did a somersault in your throat. Once you have felt it, it is unmistakable. This coordination is irreplaceable as a way to define for yourself the difference between the registers, and to ensure that you are able to isolate each one separate from the other.

Note: If you are interested in practice CDs to help with these and many other exercises, visit www.VocalArtistry.com for a complete line of training CDs.

Developing the Head Voice for Women

I would describe about half of the women I have worked with over my career as *chest-voice* singers. The chest voice is where they have done almost all of their singing, and usually they despise their head voice. They only go into their head voice when they absolutely have to and usually it's only by accident. When this happens, they feel their sound loses all strength and depth—so completely that they want to apologize to anyone who had to hear it! They are notorious for slipping guitar players bribes under the table to have them capo songs down into keys that allow them to perform the entire song in chest voice.

Most of the chest-voice singers that I have worked with have had little or no training. They have spent their lives singing in modern styles that use very little head voice (if any at all) and have not sung in choirs or pursued vocal instruction. Female chest-voice singers often avoid private training because they aren't interested in performing classical music.

The process of developing the head voice for ladies is usually pretty straightforward—just start using it. The more you use it, the stronger it will be. It is really primarily about repetition.

The one adjustment that feels foreign to the chest-voice singer who is developing the head voice is the openness in the throat that head voice requires, especially in the upper range. Because these singers are often opposed to singing in a classical style, they try to belt their head voice with the same coordination that they use in their chest voice, and this simply doesn't work. The tone should be free, open, relaxed, and supported, and if you are doing it correctly it should feel as though the sound is releasing out the top of your head. In the head voice, you will feel the soft palate lift. The soft palate is the roof of the mouth in the very back. Run your tongue along the roof of your mouth from front to back. Just past the halfway point you will feel a ridge. Everything behind that ridge is called the soft palate, and you can feel how the roof of the mouth behind that point is no longer hard bone structure, but soft and fleshy. The soft palate and the area behind it in the back of your throat will lift and expand as you sing in head voice. It is often helpful to think of using an internal smile as you sing in head voice, or even of raising your eyebrows. Sopranos are notorious for this smiley, happy look on their faces when they sing, especially in the upper part of their range, because this adjustment helps lift the resonance area that allows them to access a pure head-voice production.

As you develop your head voice, it may help to keep in mind that the classical tone of an open throat doesn't have to be forceful and dramatic like you would hear from an opera singer performing Wagner. The classical tone that will be most helpful for the modern worship singer to develop is more like the light and lyric tone you hear from Enya, Charlotte Church, or Celtic Women. Use these singers as a guide for the kind of tone you should be striving to produce as you vocalize. The tone is pure, light, ethereal, and free from tension.

Here is an exercise that will help you to develop the head voice.

Figure 4.7. Isolated Head Voice Exercise (Women)

Audio Example 4.3. Isolated Head Voice Exercise (Women)

In addition to your vocal exercises, songs that exercise your head voice are a great supplement to your vocal workout. Since modern worship is a chest voice–dominated style, it will be difficult to find worship songs for the female voice that will challenge you and help you to build your head voice. Instead, sing along with recordings of male worship leaders, and sing a full octave above where they are singing. This will allow you to sing songs in the style you want to work in, but also provide a good workout for your head voice.

Why Develop Head Voice?

Why is it important for the modern singer to develop head voice? Most modern music, including worship, is sung almost exclusively in the chest voice. If you are a chest-voice singer, you may be wondering why you should emphasize singing in a production that you will rarely use, especially when it is one that you feel so uncomfortable with.

- Improved Tone. The benefits begin with an improvement in the quality of your tone. Most chest-voice singers have a forced quality to their voice. They sound great on tunes that rock, but singing with a pretty tone is challenging. Developing the head voice will allow you to bring a sweeter quality to your tone without all of the drive and force associated with a full-on chest-voice production.

- Ability to Use Head Voice. Developing the head voice will also allow you to smoothly transition between the registers and incorporate more head voice into your worship. Singers like Kari Jobe and Christy Nockels are wonderful examples of female worship leaders who incorporate this technique and bring head voice into their singing as a beautiful contrast to chest voice. They also use the head voice to help them sing higher than the chest voice would allow. Do you need some help pulling off those Chris Tomlin songs that your worship leader keeps choosing that stretch your range out of its comfort zone? Developing your head voice and incorporating it into your singing will help!

- Blended Chest Voice. Probably the greatest benefit in developing your head voice comes in the final process of register development, chest blend. This technique requires balanced strength between chest voice and head voice, and is the secret to extending your chest voice range above your break. There will be more discussion about this below.

Developing the Chest Voice for Women

I have worked with just as many women who are in need of developing the chest voice as I have those who need to develop the head voice. Often times, head-voice singers have come from classical training or a strong choral background. These environments often encourage female singers to sing only in their head voice, and some instructors go so far as to forbid their students to use chest voice at all. I've even heard of some conservative institutions that place a moral stigma on using the chest voice. They say that chest voice is what singers use when they sing in smoky bars on Friday and Saturday nights, and so their singers are pretty sure they could go to hell for using chest voice.

This prejudice against chest voice can be a difficult thing for some singers to reconcile, especially if they are interested in singing in modern styles. Pop, rock, blues and gospel are all chest voice–dominated styles. Modern worship is no different. The days of Twila Paris and Sandi Patty have come and gone. If you turn your radio on to any station playing modern music, you're going to hear almost all chest voice. In order to be successful and sound legitimate in modern styles (including worship), you have to develop the ability to sing in your chest voice.

I had a colleague who studied at the same undergraduate institution that I did. She graduated with a degree in vocal performance and shortly after graduating got hired for a studio gig in Indianapolis. She lived in Chicago, and so she drove the three and a half hours to Indy to do the session. Shortly into the job the producer came out from the control room and said, "Honey, when you've found your chest voice let me know," and that was the end of the session for her. It was a long three-and-a-half-hour drive back to Chicago to sit with the realization that she had just invested four years of her life and enough money to buy a house without receiving training that prepared her to compete in the field that she wanted to go into. Without a chest voice, she was lacking an aspect of technique that is simply nonnegotiable for the modern singer.

Discovering Chest Voice

Many head-voice singers don't even realize that they aren't able to sing in chest voice. The head voice has tremendous potential for volume and intensity, and can do a pretty good job of disguising itself as a chest voice, especially if it's had years of practice at it. But the tone, the quality, and the characteristics of chest voice are just different from those of head voice. It is truly a different instrument. No matter how hard you blow on a clarinet, it is never going to sound like a trumpet, and the same is true for head voice. Chest voice is not just a head voice that you are blowing into really hard; it is a completely different vocal production, involving different muscles and coordination, and it produces an unmistakably different sound.

So how do you know if you are singing in head voice when you intend to sing in chest voice? Here are some indications that you are singing in head voice:

1. The voice gets lighter as you carry it lower.
2. You aren't able to belt on the same pitches that you hear other singers belt. If you find that the C, D, E, and even possibly F and G toward the top of the treble clef staff are your strongest notes, you're singing in a really strong (and possibly blended) head voice, not chest voice.
3. You go from the lowest part of your range to the highest, and you don't feel any noticeable transition in your voice, and there is no break or crack at any point.
4. You are unable to find a yodel click from the highest notes that you think are chest voice, up into head voice.

Working with singers who rarely (or never) sing in chest voice, and walking them through the process of developing chest voice, is challenging. There aren't many aspects of technique that are more difficult, and I think this one probably takes the prize. It's tough!

Probably the most difficult aspect of the process is that when head-voice singers begin to develop chest voice, they almost always hate the new sound that they are creating. The reason for this is that when the chest-voice muscles are weak, the only way to get them to function and build strength is to sing loud—very, very loud! When head-voice singers describe this new sound they use words like "obnoxious," "brash," and "shouty," saying, "I don't feel like I'm singing, I feel like I'm hollering!" When I hear these descriptions, I know we're on the right track!

The mark of a strong and developed chest voice is not how loudly you can sing in it, it's how softly you can sing in it. The stronger the chest voice gets, the greater the ability to back away on all of the intensity and volume. Eventually dynamic contrast and a very sweet tone quality will begin to emerge from the chest voice. But when you start out, you're hollering! If you try to take any of the volume and intensity away, you will simply crack into the more developed head voice.

The best way I have found to kickstart this new production is to use a shout as a reference point. Try standing up straight, and, with a wide-open throat and good, deep breath support, shout, "Hah." Notice that I didn't use the word "yell" or "scream," I used the word "shout." Don't shy away from the volume at all. And do not underestimate the amount of energy and intensity you will have to use to engage the chest voice. Don't shout across the room, shout to the guy in the parking lot of the next building over, and pretend he's the guy who cut you off in traffic last week. "Hah!!!" Now that we have that shouted "hah" as a reference point, the trick is to begin with the shout, and then sing a scale without any change at all to the tone. Don't think of this as singing, because if you've never used your chest voice, this isn't going to feel like any singing you've ever done. You are essentially shouting on pitch. So start with the shout, and then transition into a five-note scale using the same tone quality you used on the shout.

I would recommend starting just below the treble clef in C major (with G as the high note) and modulating by half steps as high as you can. Typically when a head-voice singer is first beginning to develop the chest voice, the highest note she can reach in this new production is around A, B, or C in the middle of the treble clef staff. Carry the exercise as high as you are able without straining or manipulating your throat, or introducing any other area of tension.

Figure 4.8. Isolated Chest Voice Exercise (Women)

Audio Example 4.4. Isolated Chest Voice Exercise (Women)

Once you've established this, repeat the exercise, only this time carry the chest voice beyond your limit, until you feel and hear the chest voice crack over into head voice. This is a critical part of defining the break and truly isolating the registers. If you are unable to get a true break or crack in the voice, chances are you are not carrying the full chest voice all the way to the break. Commit yourself to a full-on chest-voice production, and then, at the very edge of what you can stand, allow the voice to flip into a head-voice production. You want to feel and hear a completely uncoordinated break in the voice—take it right over the edge of the cliff. It will sound terrible, and I'm sure you will be horrified by what you hear, but it is essential to define this limit, and to know where the true end of the chest voice is.

Now, I can already hear the outrage of classical voice instructors all over the world preparing to burn me at the stake for this heresy. But finding the isolated chest voice is essential in order to build range in the upper chest voice and eventually to discover the chest blend. If the singer is always backing away from the full engagement of the chest voice at the highest notes in the chest voice range in order to smooth out the transition into head voice, the muscles for those highest notes in chest voice are never engaged and will never be developed to their full capacity. You have to take chest voice right up to the edge of the cliff and then fall off of it for this process to work. And you will only achieve the chest blend if you have a fully developed chest voice to blend. You can't blend dirt and water to make mud if you don't have any dirt. As we will discuss in the section on blending the registers, the chest voice must be balanced in strength with the head voice in order to find a blended production that is viable for modern styles—but more on that later.

There are a couple of guidelines that singers must follow in order to protect themselves from the vocal damage that my classical colleagues are so concerned about. Many an otolaryngologist has purchased a vacation home on the Mexican Riviera thanks to chest-voice singers who have completely blown out their voices and are in need of their services. Misuse of the chest voice is probably the most common cause of vocal damage. The chest voice must be developed intelligently and responsibly, and these are the three keys for a lifetime of healthy singing in your chest voice:

1. Do not carry pure chest voice above the break. You want to carry it right up to the break, but at the point where you are required to manipulate the voice in order to sing higher, don't do it! Allow the chest voice to break over into head voice at that point, but do not carry a full, isolated chest-voice production above your voice's natural break. The only safe way

to carry a chest-voice production over the break is by using chest blend, but we're not there yet.

2. The rules of vocal freedom apply just as much to chest voice as they do to head voice. Do not use tension to force the chest-voice production. Keep the throat open and relaxed and use diaphragmatic support to provide energy for the chest voice.
3. Because your only option when you first start is a full-on, loud and obnoxious production, this will be exhausting on your voice. I have worked with singers who could sing in chest voice for only two or three minutes before their voices reached the point of fatigue. Recognize the signs of fatigue (hoarseness or scratchiness in the throat, loss of pitch control, cracking), and as soon as you feel these effects, take a break. Type-A personalities and overachievers, beware! You only risk serious vocal damage by pushing your voice beyond this point. It will not speed up the development process for you. Take a complete vocal break for a minimum of twenty minutes, possibly an hour, possibly half a day—and it may be that you're done for the day at that point. Rest until your voice feels like it's back to normal, and then come back to it, still cautiously monitoring the signs of fatigue.

With these parameters in place you are free to dive in and begin the process of developing your chest voice. Have fun with it! Go for it! You probably aren't going to like the sound your voice is producing, but don't let that slow you down from regularly exercising this part of your voice. You want to be doing vocal exercises on a daily basis, and ideally a number of times throughout the day, as much as your vocal endurance will allow. It is better to practice this area of technique four times a day for five minutes than to push through one practice session of twenty minutes. Regular, consistent conditioning of these muscles is the key to development.

In addition to regular vocal exercises, find songs that you can sing in your chest voice, and put together a practice CD of them. The challenge is finding songs that don't go too high, as most professionals have developed the ability to carry the chest blend above the break. It is also helpful to find songs that are upbeat and rowdy, since the only version of chest voice you will have for awhile is going to feel like you're shouting on pitch! "Enough" and "Never Alone" by Barlow Girl, "Stay" by Sugarland, and "Run to You" by Lady Antebellum are a great place to start. Keep the top note below a B in the middle of the treble clef staff.

I have seen singers fight this process, and go kicking and screaming every step of the way. They practice inconsistently because they don't like the sound or the feel of this new production, and they stay stuck where they are, sometimes for years. Jump into the deep end. Get to work. Practice consistently. Don't shy away from the volume or intensity required to exercise the isolated chest voice; exercise regularly and intelligently, avoiding tension, recognizing the signs of fatigue; and resist the urge to carry pure chest voice above the break. There is a Promised Land on the other side of this challenging process, and it is well worth the journey!

Developing the Head Voice (Falsetto) for Men

So, guys, I will take the mystery out of it for you right now. You are a chest-voice singer. I haven't had a guy yet in over twenty years of coaching singers who walked into my studio and was stuck in head voice and unable to sing consistently in the chest voice. Guys sing in chest voice; it's what we do. That doesn't mean that you don't have some serious work to do in strengthening your chest voice and expanding your chest voice range, but the register that is the most underdeveloped is the head voice or falsetto (different words describing the same thing).

The challenge I have in motivating men to develop their ability to sing in their head voice is that in modern styles men rarely use it. And if all you ever sing is worship music, you may never sing in head voice when you sing songs. None of the mainstream male worship leaders use head voice in any of their songs: Paul Baloche, Chris Tomlin, Matt Redman, and so on. So why is it important to develop the head voice if you are never going to use it?

The value of developing head voice becomes clear in the third step in the process of developing the registers: the blend. Most guys sing exclusively in their chest voice, with no assistance or blend from the head voice, even on the highest notes in their range. They drive up a sound that gets louder and louder, and more and more pushed, forced, and strained, until eventually at the very top of their range they crack over into a pathetic, airy head-voice sound. Have you ever heard recordings of yourself singing at the top of your range and it sounded like you were just yelling?

It is critical for the quality of tone in our upper chest-voice range, and for our vocal health and longevity, to blend and coordinate some assistance from the head voice into our chest voice. This will allow us to extend our range and improve the sound of our voice, and it will protect our voice and allow us to sing for a lifetime in a healthy, sustainable way. We'll talk more in the next section about how to develop the blend, but before we can hope to blend, we first need to develop a head voice that is balanced in strength with the chest voice.

Since so little of our music is written for us to sing in head voice as men, it's no wonder our head voice is so underdeveloped. We develop the head voice only through a very intentional choice to set aside time to exercise it. The most important thing to do is to just get into the gym and start working out with vocal exercises. Your head voice is the unused register, so the muscles are weak and underdeveloped; just start using them. The more time you spend singing in the head voice, the stronger it will get.

When most of the guys I've worked with begin developing their head voice, they have a thin, whiny tone—something that sounds like a really bad imitation of the Bee Gees or the Beach Boys. The tone is pinched, their larynx is high in the throat, the corners of the mouth spread out wide to the sides, and often there is a fair amount of neck tension that causes the chin to rise. This is not the approach that will be most helpful as you develop the head voice.

The tone we are looking for is a deep, full tone. The larynx should stay down; the neck should stay relaxed; the jaw should drop, creating a vertical shape to the mouth; and you should feel a wide-open space in the back of your throat like you just swallowed an orange. The tone will sound ridiculous, much like Julia Child's. I am not suggesting that your head voice should sound like this when you do use it in a song, but for the purposes of developing strength and creating space for the head voice to expand, this is the approach you want to use in all of your exercises.

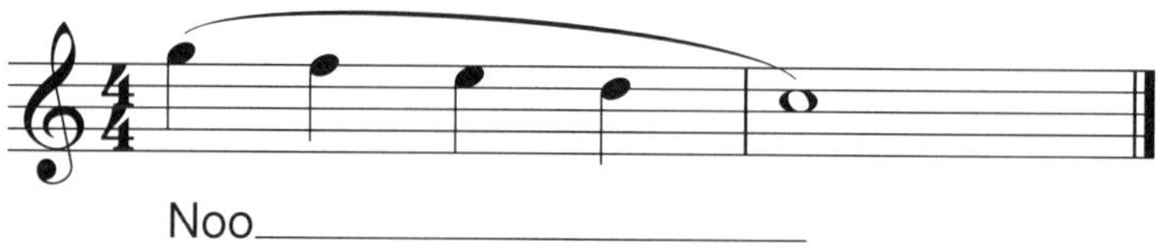

Figure 4.9. Isolated Head Voice Exercise (Men)

Audio Example 4.5. Isolated Head Voice Exercise (Men)

In addition to regular vocal exercises, a great way to supplement your workout is to find some songs that will require you to sing in your head voice. I would recommend finding some recordings of women who sing in a low female range. Female worship leaders are a great option, because they generally sing low and won't be using an extensive range or vocal acrobatics that will be too demanding. Once you have chosen your music, sing along with the female vocalist up in her range in your head voice. I recommend compiling a CD with ten songs that you can sing along with, and playing it in your car and around the house, singing along with it throughout your day. It's a great way to get in some extra reps between workouts and to continue strengthening those head voice muscles.

Developing the Chest Voice for Men

As we've already discussed, guys know how to sing in their chest voice. But even though they've spent their entire lives doing just that, they may still be missing out on the full strength and freedom the chest voice has the potential to achieve. This is particularly true for the modern worship singer.

Modern worship is almost always sung in a pop/rock style. The tone required for this style is generally thin and performed with a slightly elevated larynx (and in some cases a very high laryngeal position). The singer who performs exclusively in this style will lack strength, depth, and range, never approaching the full potential of the voice.

The other dynamic with modern worship is that it is intentionally dumbed-down music for the masses. It is written so that every person in the congregation can sing along with it. The range is not challenging (except for some of those Chris Tomlin songs that need to be lowered for most congregations), and the melodies are simple and "singable," avoiding awkward phrasing or interval jumps. It is not demanding music to sing. Because of this, it is very easy for the muscles in the voice to atrophy if worship is the only environment in which you exercise your voice.

Most men whom I have worked with are in serious need of getting their chest voice into the gym, throwing some challenging weights on the bar, and getting those muscles bulked up. This happens best by singing in a classical style. The full, deep, and resonant tone required in a classical setting creates space and develops strength in the voice in a way that singing in modern styles never will. Daily practice, with exercises that modulate by half step through the range, is the critical foundation to build on. Here are the qualities of this production that are essential:

1. The jaw should be dropped, and the vowel open. This may feel overly exaggerated for the modern worship singer, but it is essential for relaxing

tension and creating the space required to generate this classical tone.

2. The tone should be rich and full, and brightly resonant at the same time. Often, singers will simply swallow the sound when trying to create a classical tone. If the sound is swallowed, it indicates that the back of the throat is closed. If the throat is open, not only will the voice be full and rich, but, since there is nothing blocking the sound as it is produced and projected, it will be free to resonate forward in the mask of the face, giving a bright ringing quality to the tone.
3. The throat should be open, which will result in a lowered larynx. Be sure to monitor the larynx when you are practicing to ensure that you are creating enough space to generate this classical tone, as discussed in the Laryngeal Tension section of the chapter on vocal freedom.
4. The classical tone we are looking for is a very energized vocal production. All of the energy for the tone must be coming from breathing and support, not from vocal strain. Make sure that you are using the breathing technique described in the chapter on breathing and support, and engaging all of the energy from the breath that you can. No wimpy singing!

Here is an exercise that you can use to strengthen the chest voice. If you sing along with the CD, try to match the tone you hear demonstrated by the singer on the recording.

Figure 4.10. Isolated Chest Voice Exercise (Men)

Audio Example 4.6. Isolated Chest Voice Exercise (Men)

Step 2: Building Overlap Between the Registers

Once the registers have been isolated, and developed independently, the next step is to build overlap between the registers. You want to work on bringing head voice down through the range, and extending chest voice up.

Building Head Voice Down

A great exercise for building head voice down is the same yodel exercise introduced in the section on isolating the registers.

This will serve as a litmus test to ensure that you are staying in head voice on the first five notes of each exercise. It will be easier as you go lower though your range to slip into chest voice. The yodel into chest voice will tell you whether or not you have been successful. If you don't get a crack in your voice, you cheated. Your goal should be to go lower in your head voice every day, and still get the yodel.

Figure 4.11. Descending Head Voice Yodel Exercise

Building Chest Voice Up

As we've already discussed, for both men and women the keys to extending the full chest voice range higher are freedom from tension, a wide-open throat, and energy from breath support. The chest voice range won't be able to expand as far upward as the head voice will be able to expand downward, but recognizing tension, expanding the throat to avoid constriction and collapse, and increasing the efficiency of low diaphragmatic breathing and support should allow you to see an increase (maybe a few half steps, maybe half an octave) in the range of the chest voice.

One Full Octave of Overlap

The goal for every singer is to have a full octave that he or she can sing with equal strength in either head voice or chest voice. That doesn't mean equal volume, as the chest voice will often be able to generate more decibels than the same pitch sung in head voice. But the control, consistency of vibrato and tone, and muscular stability should be matched in both head voice and chest voice over a full octave!

For many singers, even stopping right there at step two in this process would change their lives vocally. Most of the singers I meet have no overlap whatsoever. The relationship between head voice and chest voice is the same as the relationship between sand and water that have been sitting in a jar: there is no relationship. The sand is on the bottom and the water is on the top, and there is a static line between the two. Many singers are familiar with this static line. For many of them there is a note name attached to this static line, and everything they sing that is north of that line has to be in head voice, and everything south of that line has to be in chest voice. So the first thing they do when they receive a new piece of music is to quickly scan through it to see what parts will be in head voice and what parts will be in chest voice and where and when they will have to make that dreaded, awkward transition between the two. Imagine a full octave, in the middle of your range, on the notes you sing the most, where you can choose head voice or chest voice as a viable option, because over that entire octave the registers are balanced in strength. For some of you, that would indeed change your life.

But we don't stop there. The final step in the process is where we cash in on the prize we've worked so hard for in the other two steps. It's the step where we grab the jar of sand and water and shake it up, because once we have an octave overlap of isolated head voice and chest voice, it's time to start finding the blend.

Step 3: Blending the Registers

The blend occurs when the voice is able to sing in a certain register (either head voice or chest voice) and add some of the muscular involvement of the other register without collapsing and giving in fully to that opposing register (as happens in the yodel flip). We end up with two versions of the blend: head blend and chest blend.

Head Blend

The head blend is a predominantly head-voice production that (physiologically speaking) brings in some of the coordination of chest voice by shortening the length of the vocal cords, expanding the thickness of the cords, and increasing the amplitude of sound generated in this vocal production. In other words, we get some of the fullness and depth that are present in chest voice, blended into the head voice. Some of my colleagues may disagree, but I don't feel there is a place for blended head voice in modern style. It is the tone that you hear most often in the voice of a classically trained female—a reinforced head voice with lots of depth and fullness and power. When I work with classically trained females we spend a great deal of time "unlearning" this vocal production. They are consistently wanting to transition into head blend in the upper part of their range when they need strength and power. That's just not what I hear on my radio, or from the people winning Grammys in modern styles. The singer needs to either choose an appropriate place in the song to float up to a light, ethereal head voice, or extend the range of her chest blend in order to generate the tone in a predominantly chest-voice production. When the modern singer uses a strong head blend as a substitute for chest voice or chest blend, it sounds honky, nasal, and trained. The listener isn't quite sure what's wrong, but even the untrained ear knows that something is not right because this tone just doesn't fit.

Chest Blend

The Promised Land for the singer is the chest blend. This is the secret for extending the chest voice over your break and up into the stratosphere of your range. Have you ever wondered how some of your favorite singers can sing so high without cracking over into a head voice or a classical-sounding head blend—or, for that matter, bleeding from the larynx? This is the secret!

Remember that I warned head-voice singers who are developing chest voice never to extend pure chest voice above the break? That warning still holds true. But if you are able to add some of the physiological function of head voice into the chest voice by extending the length of the vocal cords, thinning out the thickness of the cords, and slightly decreasing the amplitude of sound, then you are using chest blend and can safely extend the chest voice above the break.

I cannot emphasize enough how critical it is to work diligently on steps one and two in this process. Everyone wants step three, the chest blend! But you simply cannot hope to find the blended chest voice unless you have first isolated each register, built up the individual strength of each one independent of the other, and built crossover between the registers (ideally a full octave that you can sing equally well in each register). Most often the chest blend is just a natural by-product of the first two steps.

Typically, I will begin working with someone and we will start isolating the registers. He or she will be doing all of the yodel exercises and exercises isolating the registers—working each register independent of the other. For months the singer will hit a certain part of his or her range and the voice will awkwardly crack between chest voice and head voice. We may see some slight increase in the range he or she can achieve before the voice cracks, but for these first months, the crack occurs consistently on the same pitch.

Then, one day, I will ask the singer to make some slight adjustments to his or her approach in the upper part of the chest voice, and in that one lesson things just click. The point where the voice has been cracking for months suddenly adjusts and the singer finds a new gear that allows him or her to shift and move right through the break. Sometimes it's only a few half steps, but I've seen people add as much as half an octave to the top of their chest voice range before they crack into head voice. Men are suddenly singing Gs, As, and Bs in the lower middle of the treble clef staff, and women are suddenly singing Cs, Ds, and Es toward the top of the treble clef staff, without breaking over into head voice.

Characteristics of Chest Blend

Steps one and two are the key to accomplishing chest blend, but anticipating the following sound qualities of chest blend can encourage the blend to emerge once the voice is ready.

1. Increased Nasality. The tone in chest blend will always have a bit of a nasal bite to it. This is not to say that the tone becomes nasal; depth and richness still characterize the sound, but added to the depth is a bright nasal resonance that is different from isolated chest voice.
2. Narrowed Focus. When the isolated chest voice is carried up through the range, the tone broadens the higher the singer goes. The resonance seems to expand and fill more of the room. However, in chest blend the tone seems to narrow as the thinning of the vocal cords changes the depth of the tone. The projection of isolated chest voice is like a wide column of sound coming out and filling a wide angle in front of the singer.

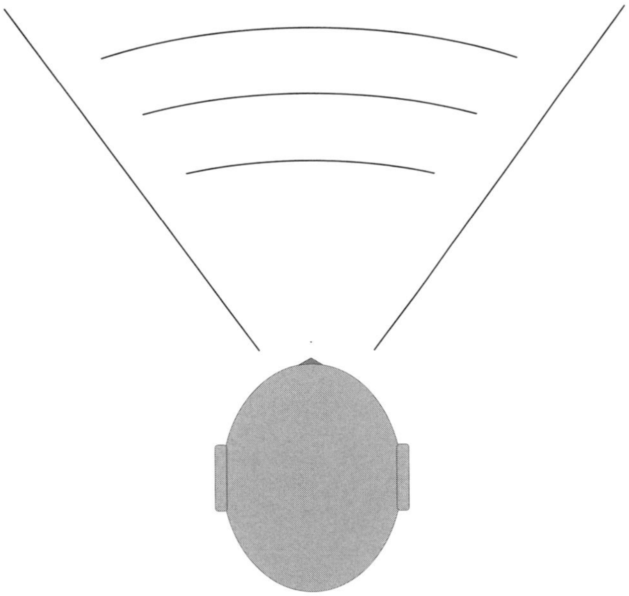

Figure 4.12. Wide Projection of Pure Chest Voice

In chest blend, the tone has a point to it, a narrow focus where the singer has the sense that the sound is all being sent to a very specific location.

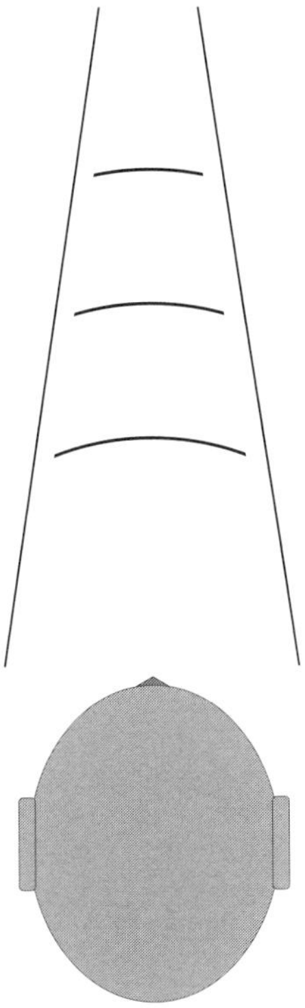

Figure 4.13. Narrow Projection of Chest Blend

3. Slightly Softer. I will never forget the first day one of my clients discovered chest blend. Even though it was over a decade ago, it left a strong impression on me. It was a light-bulb moment where everything we'd been working on for months finally clicked, and suddenly her range extended into places it had never found before without cracking into head voice. We stopped the exercise and she immediately knew what she'd done—she had discovered chest blend. After the laughs and the high-fives she looked at me and said, "It's like decaffeinated chest voice!" Brilliant! That's exactly right. It's chest voice, no question about it, but it's a milder version of chest voice that doesn't carry with it all the electricity and volume we experience in isolated chest voice. And, more than that, the tone will slightly mellow and relax. Usually the first time a singer hears the new production back from a recording, he or she can immediately tell that not only has the range increased, but the quality of sound has improved. The singer no longer requires the force of the isolated chest voice in order to sing that high in the range.

Here is an exercise that will encourage the blended chest voice to emerge. Incorporate the three characteristics mentioned above as you sing through the exercise, especially as the range increases.

Figure 4.14. Chest Blend Exercise

For Women:

Audio Example 4.7. Chest Blend Exercise (Women)

For Men:

Audio Example 4.8. Chest Blend Exercise (Men)

Benefits to Vocal Health

Developing the chest blend is essential to the vocal health and longevity of the modern singer. Nothing will tax the voice more than barreling pure chest voice up through the range. The blended chest voice is the only safe way to extend a chest-voice production above the break, and it is simply a much better sound. Once you have found this gear, it will be the production you use for the vast majority of your modern singing.

We have already discussed how the range will increase with chest blend, but you'll find your endurance increases as well. Using only one register is exhausting! This is true in every part of our body where we were created to use two sets of muscles, but choose to only use one. Imagine if someone asked you to leave your house, walk to the nearest grocery store, buy two full bags of groceries, and take them home. Depending on how close the nearest grocery store is, this could require some effort, but for the most part it's no big deal, right? Well, imagine if you did this, but you decided to use only your right leg to hop all the way to the store, around the store as you buy the groceries, and then all the way back home. That's a very different experience! You're going to return sweaty, injured, and possibly bleeding as a result, and it's going to take your body days to recover from what you just did to it.

Singers do this to their voices all the time. They sing in isolated chest voice, with no assistance from their head voice. If you are going to be successful as a modern singer, you need chest blend. It will protect your voice from the fatigue and potential damage that consistently singing in isolated chest voice over years can cause, it will improve your tone, and it will extend your range.

And the great news is that this is not a technique that is reserved for a "chosen few." This is anatomy and physiology. Every voice is designed in this way and has the potential to develop the ability to blend the chest voice with just enough head voice to gain all of these tremendous benefits. But it doesn't happen by itself. It takes hard work, commitment, determination, and consistency. But there is an amazing reward on the other side of all of that hard work and investment, and it will revolutionize your life as a singer!

5

Developing a Vocal Workout Plan

So you're motivated to develop your voice and move beyond those limitations that have been holding you back from discovering your potential. You realize it's going to take hard work and discipline to do it, and you're ready to go! So, what is the best way to practice? How can you best utilize your time in order to get the maximum impact from your hard work?

You can have all of the motivation and discipline in the world, and yet if you are not clear on how to best approach your practice time, you can end up spinning your tires and wasting valuable time and energy. You can even be very clear on what areas of development you need to focus on, but if you don't have the right game plan and approach, you may not see the progress in those areas that you desire.

This chapter will outline the structure and approach that you need in order to maximize your vocal workout so that you know exactly what and how you need to practice.

Time

You are a vocal athlete, and you need to approach your training in much the same way that athletes approach their workouts. Time and consistency are critical in the world of vocal development, just as they are in the world of professional athletics. If you want to develop your ability and see growth and progress, it's not going to work to take the week off and then put in a crash course beginning Saturday morning in order to get yourself ready to sing on Sunday. Vocal development involves muscle building, coordination, and endurance, and all of these take time and consistency.

The baseline you want to shoot for is 20–30 minutes, three to four times per week, of vocal technique exercises specifically targeting the areas of development most critical for your voice. This is not 20–30 minutes of pulling out your favorite karaoke CDs, or sitting down with your guitar or piano and playing through songs that give you warm fuzzies and make you feel good about your voice. It's 20–30 minutes, three to four times per week, of getting into the vocal gym and singing vocal exercises (not songs) that will work out and develop your voice.

Allow time above and beyond that to develop style and to prepare for services and rehearsals so that you can focus exclusively on technique building during your workouts. Any less than this level of consistency and you simply won't see the improvement and growth that you desire.

It's actually a very similar time frame to what you would hear from a doctor if you asked how long and how often you should exercise to keep your body in good cardiovascular shape. Remember, you are a vocal athlete and you need to log the time in order to see the results.

Environment

When deciding on the best environment for your workouts, here are some important factors to help you get the most out of your practice time:

1. Find a place where you can focus completely on your voice without interruption or distraction. Much of the progress you will make, especially as your voice continues to improve and your technique becomes more advanced, will involve subtle adjustments that will require all of your attention as you fine-tune them and lock them into your muscle memory. Practicing while you are multitasking or constantly being interrupted will significantly slow your progress. Try to set aside time where the rest of the world stops for 20–30 minutes and all that you are focusing on is your voice.

One of the most popular activities to combine with your vocal workout is driving. It's a great way to utilize the time you have, right? Well, yes and no. In the car, you are preoccupied with other things going on around you (at least, I hope you are), you can't watch yourself sing in the mirror most of the time, and your posture likely isn't conducive to proper breathing coordination and support. Another aspect of singing in the car that creates problems is that you are singing above street and engine noise. Have you ever driven down the freeway at 60 miles an hour, singing along with the song that's playing on your car stereo, and all of a sudden traffic comes to a screeching halt and you notice your music is blaring in the car? Did your music suddenly get a lot louder? No, everything around you got quieter and now you can hear how loud the music actually was the entire time. This is the same thing that happens when you sing and drive. It will require you to over-sing, and could encourage bad habits, establishing technique that could actually be more harmful than helpful. Is practicing in the car a total waste? No. But be aware of the challenges that come with that environment and make sure that you are practicing outside of the car as much as you are practicing in it.

2. Use a mirror! As we discussed in the chapter on vocal freedom, the only way for you to recognize some of the bad habits that are showing up in your technique is to see them. You may not notice that your jaw is thrusting out when you get louder, or that your chin is rising in your upper range, because it feels so natural—you've been doing it your entire life. And the only way you'll be able to see it and correct it is if you are watching yourself in the mirror. The key word there is *watch*. In my studio I have a giant, seven-foot mirror. Everyone who has ever walked into my studio can see his or her entire body in it. And yet it amazes me how often at the precise time the bad habit that needs to be identified shows up, the singer's eyes look away for a moment. It's almost as if people know they're about to get busted, and by looking away they are saying, "Who, me? I didn't do it! I saw nothing!" Have a mirror, stand in front of it, and actually use it!
3. Record yourself. Be sure to have some type of recording device in your practice environment. None of us has an accurate sense of what we actually sound like. Adjustments that you think work and sound great will turn out not to be useful at all, and other adjustments that feel awkward and sound terrible to you may be exactly the vocal production you've been looking

for. Whenever you need an objective perspective on different adjustments you are making with your voice, or new aspects of technique that you are experimenting with, record yourself!

Program

Your regular vocal workout should be very similar to an athlete who is cross training. Every time you work out, your program should have diversity and balance to it. I would not recommend spending 20–30 minutes trying to eliminate one aspect of vocal tension, or working exclusively on the chest voice. It is best for your practice session to have some variety in regard to the types of vocal issues you are targeting. To maximize your time investment, you want to develop a workout plan that includes a warm-up, targeted and balanced technique exercises, and a cooldown.

Here is a recommended flow for your vocal workout. Follow this routine in sequential order from beginning to end.

Warm-up Exercises

Begin with one or two exercises that gradually and conservatively warm up your voice—like a runner would stretch out. These exercises should be moderate in vocal range and dynamics: not too high or too low, and not too loud or too soft.

A simple three-note scale (Do, Re, Mi, Re, Do) can be a great way to begin your warm-up. Try humming, with the throat open and the resonance vibrating forward in the nose and mouth. Modulate the scale up and down by half-steps, keeping the exercise in a comfortable range.

Breathing and Support Exercises

Even a seasoned veteran needs consistent reinforcement of the proper breathing and support technique. Singers get lazy with this aspect of technique and forget to approach it with the necessary consistency and focus. We depend on breathing and support to provide all the energy for successful singing. But there are so many other things that we are focused on while we are singing that breathing often gets lost in the mix. Practice at least one breathing exercise and one support exercise every day so that it becomes a subconscious and automatic aspect of your singing.

Audio Example 5.1. Breathing Exercise

Audio Example 5.2. Support Exercise

Freedom Exercises

You need to be very clear on exactly which areas of tension are hindering your technique. Every time you practice you should work on one exercise specifically targeting each of those areas of tension separately. Just focus on one area of tension at a time. It is a good idea to have some exercises that are challenging for you to do, and some that are easy and consistently help you find a place of open relaxation and freedom. Sing the following exercises to help alleviate neck, jaw, laryngeal, tongue, lip, face, and cheek tension.

Audio Example 5.3. Neck Tension Exercise

Audio Example 5.4. Jaw Tension Exercise

Audio Example 5.5. Laryngeal Tension Exercise

Audio Example 5.6. Lip, Face, and Cheek Tension Exercise

Audio Example 5.7. Tongue Tension Exercise

Register Separation Exercises

Before isolating the registers and working on building the strength and range of the head voice and chest voice, it is important to do an exercise that will help you separate the registers using the yodel flip. The most important thing in this exercise is getting a defined click—and it is much better to establish a strong flip on one or two modulations than to sing through an entire exercise across your range without a true break. Begin by defining the yodel flip on whatever octave jump is easiest, and then modulate up and down by half steps to the extent that you are able to maintain a consistent flip.

Audio Example 5.8. Octave Yodel Exercise 1

Audio Example 5.9. Octave Yodel Exercise 2

Head Voice Isolation Exercises

Regardless of whether you are a head-voice or chest-voice singer, you should do at least one exercise that will isolate your head voice and allow you to exercise the entire range of this register.

For Women:

Audio Example 5.10. Isolated Head Voice Exercise (Women)

For Men:

Audio Example 5.11. Isolated Head Voice Exercise (Men)

Chest Voice Isolation Exercises

Work on exercises that will strengthen the chest voice range. Be aware of how high you are carrying the chest voice every day, and try to gradually over time extend this range.

For Women:

Audio Example 5.12. Isolated Chest Voice Exercise (Women)

For Men:

Audio Example 5.13. Isolated Chest Voice Exercise (Men)

Chest Blend Exercises

These exercises should only be incorporated once you have achieved balance in the strength of the isolated chest voice and head voice. Once the registers are balanced (as described in the previous chapter), you can begin to incorporate exercises designed to extend the chest voice range above the break by using the chest blend.

For Women:

Audio Example 5.14. Chest Blend Exercise (Women)

For Men:

Audio Example 5.15. Chest Blend Exercise (Men)

Cooldown Exercises

Very similar to a warm-up exercise, your cooldown exercises should involve moderate range and dynamics. If your workout has involved extensive chest voice or chest blend work, it is a good idea to incorporate an exercise that will bring your head voice down throughout your range.

Every couple of months you need to go back and modify your workout. Choose new exercises that will challenge areas of further development, and take a break on some of the exercises that are becoming easy. As in athletic training, variety is good for your muscular development and coordination. To expand your repertoire of vocal exercises beyond what is offered on the accompanying CD, visit www.VocalArtistry.com for a full line of vocal training CDs.

Follow this order from start to finish, as the exercises and technique build on each other and will set your voice up for greater success as you move from one area of focus to the next. Give extra emphasis to areas that you know need additional attention. For example, if you need to develop your chest voice, do twice as many chest voice exercises as you do exercises in other areas of technique so that your chest voice gets the extra workout that it needs.

As you practice, the goal is not to just plow through every exercise and move on to the next one. As soon as you run into a problem area, stop! Back up a few modulations and come at that same section again, making some adjustments with your approach. A great deal of your improvement in singing will come when you change your technique and reprogram the muscle memory. Barreling through the exercises will only reinforce bad technique and limitations unless you recognize problem areas, back up, change the way you are approaching things, and find a new technique that works.

Record Yourself

None of us have any idea how we really sound while we are singing, unless we are singing with a mic and a pair of headphones that delivers our sound directly to our ears. Even then we don't hear the natural acoustics that everyone else hears when we sing in a room. Have you ever recorded your voice mail, listened back, and wondered who that is talking on your phone? It's you! It's just that we don't hear ourselves the way we really sound to others. Most of what we hear of our voice is internal vibration, and very little of it is actually bouncing around the room and entering our ears the way others hear our voice.

Because of this, it can be very helpful to record yourself while you are practicing. This is especially true when you are making new adjustments and trying a different approach. Record yourself as you sing these sections and allow what you hear on the recording to help you determine whether the adjustments you make work or not, rather than relying on your perception of your voice as you sing.

Eating and Drinking Before You Sing

Singers are always asking me what they can and can't eat before they sing. In general, you want to eat healthy all the time, since the healthier your whole body is, the healthier your voice will be. Beyond that, there really aren't any major dietary rules you must follow as a singer, except in the 90 minutes prior to the time you sing. As you approach the time when you need your voice to be at its best, it is a good idea to stay away from dairy, sugar, caffeine, alcohol, and some cold remedies.

Dairy products will coat your throat and create phlegm. Sugar will also coat your throat. Caffeine and alcohol are dehydrators, and it's critical that you be well hydrated in order to sing at your best. Medicines that contain antihistamines will also dry out your voice. Any medication with throat-numbing ingredients should be avoided; while it may help your throat feel better, since you can't feel the irritation, you also won't feel yourself doing anything that could be damaging it. It's like treating a sports injury with Novocain and continuing to play: it makes the injury worse because you can't feel the damage you are doing to it. Pain protects us from causing more harm to our body by showing us our limits. It is also a good idea to avoid heavy meals right before singing, since the breathing technique you will be using will involve your diaphragm aggressively pressing against your stomach and intestines, which isn't very comfortable with a pot roast and potatoes dropped in there.

The most important thing to have before you sing is water. Hydration is key to your larynx and vocal cords coordinating properly, and even helps increase endurance, so start drinking a lot of water in the 90 minutes prior to singing. A good way to monitor adequate hydration is the color of your urine. If it isn't clear and colorless, then turn the faucet back on and have a few more glasses. It's a good idea to start tapering the amount of water that you drink in the final 30 minutes or so before you sing, though, so you won't need to cut the final two songs of your set and run off stage for a break.

Singing and Illness

If it feels like it is more difficult to sing when you are sick, that's because it is! The most important thing to do is to not get sick in the first place. Every singer should have an arsenal of trusted immune-boosting remedies on hand so that at the first sign of even the slightest cold, you are on it! Products like Airborne and Emergen-C are great, vitamin-packed supplements with lots of antioxidants. Herbal supplements like echinacea, and a number of products by a company called WishGarden Herbs, are great immune boosters as well. Nothing replaces good hydration (drink lots and lots of water) and rest (get lots and lots of sleep).

Sometimes though, even with all of our best attempts at staying healthy, we still end up getting sick! Often times, illness doesn't affect the vocal cords and singers are still able to perform close to their best while they are sick. I've heard singers give amazing performances even with a terrible head cold and a fever. This isn't going to work, however, if our cold travels out of our head and we begin to feel the effects in our throat. Congestion in the chest or throat that causes coughing is the factor that affects us the most. Coughing is an extremely violent physical activity in the larynx that causes the vocal cords to swell. As soon as the vocal cords are swollen, we've moved into a different category as singers. The medical term laryngitis (or literally *swelling of the larynx*) describes this dynamic. At this point, you have a vocal injury and the best thing you can do is to rest your voice.

Sometimes, however, the show must go on. If this is the case, one of the best things you can do is to steam your vocal cords. You do this by boiling a pot of water. Lean over the pot of water, place a towel over your head, and breathe in the hot steam through a wide-open mouth. Be careful not to get too close to the steam and scald the back of your throat. Also, if you begin to feel dizzy at all, take the towel off your head and stand up. Passing out into a pot of boiling water isn't any good for your voice, or anything else for that matter! Inhaling this warm, moist air can help alleviate some of the swelling in your vocal cords and reduce the amount of hoarseness you are experiencing.

You walk a very thin line when you sing while you are sick. If you push your voice too hard and plow through it, you risk damaging your voice. I have friends, professional singers, who have developed vocal nodules because they forced themselves to sing while they were sick. Six months of complete vocal rest (you can't even talk), and some pretty intense vocal rehab when you start to return to singing are too high a price to pay for that one performance. Pay attention to your voice and listen to the signals it is giving you, and know when it's time to call in the understudy.

6

Vocal Style

Vocal style is one of the most powerful tools we have to help us express our hearts through song. Style is the palette of colors that we use to express emotion. When style is used at its best, we capture the essence of a song, connect our hearts to what we are singing, and find a full spectrum of colors that will communicate to our congregations. Style not only allows others to hear the language of the heart, but invites them to engage their hearts in the same way. But style can alienate and distance our congregations as much as it can invite and engage them. The right song, the right message, and the wrong style can render all of our efforts in rehearsal and preparation (and even in vocal development) a profound waste of time. Our voice can sound amazing, and we can develop all of the range, dynamic control, and technical ability in the world, but if we do not have control over style, we may as well be a pastor at a church in Texas, preaching in Japanese. That pastor could have passion and skill, and the right heart and motivation, but people just aren't going to get it. The inability to effectively use style can be just as much of a hindrance to our ministry in worship.

For most singers I begin working with, style is an elusive aspect of singing that they feel they have very little control over. They would explain style as the unique quality that defines their voice. It's what you hear when they sing—it's their style. Other people on their worship team have their own style. Someone on their team sounds really good on a certain type of song because that is their style. Another person sounds best on another type of song because that is their style. But style isn't something they feel they have any control over. Style is what defines them.

But this is not the case for those vocal artists who see style as a tool bag of resources that help them communicate their hearts through their voices. Style serves vocal artists but does not define them. Style is the palette of colors that they get to use as they create a work of art, painting a picture and communicating a message through song.

So how do we make that shift? How can we develop the ability to be served by style rather than defined by it? Can style be learned, or do you just do the best you can with what you've got?

Breaking Down the Mystery of Vocal Style

The first step in mastering style is to break style down into manageable pieces. We all have a broad understanding of style. We like certain styles and dislike others. We recognize when we move from one stylistic genre to another. But what are the specific characteristics that really define style? Nearly all of what defines style can be broken down into four stylistic tools:

- Diction
- Tone Color
- Vibrato
- Pitch Fluctuation

We will break style down, look at each of these defining characteristics, and discuss how we can develop control and mastery over each area. As you gain control over these tools, your palette will expand and style will become an invaluable resource in helping you express your heart through song.

Different Types of Singers

In the church, I have found there to be two different types of singers who need to work on their stylistic ability: what I will call the untrained singer and the choral singer.

Untrained Singer

Most often, the untrained singer performs in a style that fits the music that is being sung in services. For the most part, these singers work in a modern style and sound pretty cool singing worship. Their difficulty comes when any stylistic adjustments are required that fall outside of the context of whatever comes naturally. They are not thinking about style, and they are not in control of style. Whatever comes out of their mouths is what they've got. Their main focus is on sounding nice, singing in tune, and remembering their words. But when they find themselves with me in a group rehearsal, or even working on a solo, and I ask them to straighten their vibrato, or to use a more hushed, breathy tone, or to bring more vibrato to a certain section, or to eliminate the breathy quality from the voice, they have no ability to make these adjustments.

The Classical/Choral Singer

I probably could have made a living by working exclusively with "recovering" classically trained singers, or singers with a strong choral background who wanted to learn how to sing modern styles. They're everywhere! This is more prevalent in the church than probably any other environment. Many singers grew up singing hymns and anthems in the church choir before the day that modern worship became the dominant style. Those singers still have great voices, and many of them have amazing hearts that connect to the messages of worship choruses with as much depth and conviction as they did when they were singing hymns. But the stylistic model that they learned to sing with doesn't work in a band-and-mic setting with new songs. I have met many singers who feel disillusioned, like there is no longer a place for them to serve. They wonder how or if they can fit in, and many have simply stepped aside and let the next generation lead the charge. I've known many of these singers who couldn't be more open and willing to grow and expand so they can use their gifts and talents to contribute to the ministry that they love, but no one is showing them how.

The Truth About Style

For both of these groups of singers, the good news is that the challenges and limitations they face are all surmountable. Using style is a learnable skill, and I've seen singers go from having no stylistic control to possessing mastery over their voices. I've also watched singers who first walked into my studio sounding dated in modern repertoire walk out months later with a cutting-edge style that sounds as cool and accessible as any "twenty-something" on their worship team.

The key is to deconstruct style, break it down into these four manageable tools, and then develop the ability to control and master each one. A full palette of colors to help you express your heart awaits.

Diction

The goal for diction in modern worship is conversational pronunciation. In other words, if you pronounce a word a certain way in speech, you need to pronounce it that same way in your singing. The way you feel vowels formed, the way the consonants are articulated, the position of the tongue, and the shape of your mouth all need to show up in your singing the same way they show up in the way you talk.

The goal that I've defined above is very different from the classical and choral model for diction. The big difference is that in classical and choral styles, singers are encouraged to modify their diction. In other words, they are required to do things differently when they sing than when they speak. What are some of those differences?

Modified Vowels

In classical and choral style the singer opens vowels wider than in everyday speech. The general rule is that everything modifies, or changes, toward "ah." Vowels are more open and vertical, meaning that the corners of the mouth should not spread to the sides, but the jaw should always drop straight down, and the space in the mouth and back of the throat should feel as close to an "ah" vowel as possible.

This is not the case in modern worship. Conversational diction requires that vowels be shaped the same way they are in speech. I can't tell you how many times I've been in rehearsal with classically trained singers working on a modern song, and had to tell them to "spread the vowel wider, don't drop your jaw, and put a little more 'twang' into it, just like you'd say it." Whenever I do, I can sense choral directors from years past rolling over in their graves.

A great exercise that will help you work on conversational diction is to alternate between speaking a phrase and singing a phrase. Simply go through the song and speak the first line, memorizing the way the vowels feel in your mouth and how the consonants are articulated with the tongue. Then sing the phrase without changing a thing. Pronounce the words with the same feeling and emphasis (or lack thereof) as you did when you were speaking. Continue alternating throughout the entire song, getting your diction closer and closer to your speech.

Untrained singers often have the opposite problem: we can't understand everything they are singing because they aren't giving enough emphasis to pronouncing the vowels and articulating the consonants. Some even close off their singing more than their speech. We don't want to go too far in adjusting this, but it's important to create enough space in the vowels for the voice to have room to project, and it's important to give enough articulation to the consonants that you can be understood.

I think it would benefit these singers to sing something a little out of their stylistic comfort zone to develop in this area. A couple of songs that will help come from my favorite Broadway musical, *West Side Story*, by Leonard Bernstein. For guys, try singing *Something's Coming*, and for the ladies, try *I Feel Pretty*. Both will require some bright articulation in order to spit out all of the words clearly, and both will provide an opportunity to open up some vowels on sustained notes and let the voice really soar. These songs will take the modern style that you are used to singing in and bring you too far in the other direction. Once this is accomplished, though, it will be easy to keep the benefits you've learned through the exercise and just reel them back a little bit to sound appropriate for modern style.

Consonants

In classical and choral style, consonants are emphasized with crisp and clear articulation, and yet the singer spends almost no time pronouncing them, using consonants only as a quick stepping-stone to the next vowel. In modern styles the singer softens the consonants, using them much more subtly, but gives those consonants more time to sound than in classical or choral music.

Diphthongs

A diphthong is a word that contains two vowel sounds that are pronounced in succession, without a consonant between them. For example, let's take a look at the word "grace."

When you break it down, the word contains the sounds "g-r-eh-ee-s." The "eh" and "ee" sounds right next to each other, without a consonant in between, create a diphthong.

In classical and choral style singers avoid the second vowel of a diphthong, spending most of their time on the first vowel only. When we speak, we give about equal emphasis to both vowels, and that is how we should approach diphthongs in modern style.

For a demonstration of the effects of using different approaches to diction, check out the video demonstration on the DVD-ROM:

Video Example 6.1. Style Demo: Diction

Tone Color

Conversational Tone

In much the same way as diction, the goal for tone in modern worship is conversational. It should be very close to the way you sound when you speak. As I mentioned earlier when we were discussing laryngeal tension in the chapter on vocal freedom, classical style requires a low larynx position, and depth and resonance in the tone. Modern worship style requires a slightly elevated larynx, which produces a thinner tone very similar to our speaking voice.

For singers who are coming from a classical or choral background where this deeper, fuller tone has been reinforced, it is important to make the adjustment to find a speech-like tone for your singing voice. I have found that the best way to develop this ability for the classically trained or choral singer is to sing along with other artists who emulate a very conversational tone. Two such singers who come to mind in the Christian music world are Chris Rice for men and Nichole Nordeman for women.

Untrained singers don't have too much of an issue in this area. The challenge for them comes in the larynx rising too high and constricting the tone, limiting range and flexibility and potentially damaging the voice. Make sure that you are exercising in a classical tone, so that when you come to your modern singing, you maintain enough fullness and strength in your tone to sound your best and protect your voice.

Breathiness

You are not going to win the Metropolitan Opera auditions, or even pass your vocal jury, by singing with an airy, breathy tone, but it is critical for the modern worship singer to be able to sing with this technique. What this requires is to add extra breath to the tone, much as you do when you whisper. I've worked with many singers who have never done this before, and it can be quite difficult for them to find this technique, let alone to grow comfortable with it.

To begin developing a breathy quality, start singing a song using only a whisper, no tone. Then gradually add more tone, but not so much that you lose the sound of the whisper. It's going to feel weird as you do this. You'll make a lot of mistakes and your voice will feel out of control. Keep at it; it's a new production, and as you become more familiar with the feel of this new technique, the control and quality will begin to lock in.

Many untrained singers have challenges on the other side of the continuum. I have worked with some singers who were unable to create a pure tone *without* a breathy quality. We don't want that extreme, either. We want the ability to sing with a breathy tone in contrast to places where we are using more of a pure tone. The goal for all aspects of style is diversity, flexibility, and contrast.

What is happening for the untrained singer who is not able to sing with a pure tone is that the muscles that seal the vocal cords together are weak and underdeveloped. In order to develop cord closure so that no extra air is escaping with the tone, the use of a glottal attack can be helpful.

A glottal attack is when you close the cords and build up pressure from underneath and then, finally, the vocal cords blow apart and begin vibrating. The glottal attack is created with the same feeling you have when you are trying to push open a heavy door that just won't budge. You lower your shoulder and make a kind of grunting noise in your throat. Then, once the door gives way, your voice lets out a release of air and tone. Try that same thing, only clamp down your throat and do not allow any air to escape. Then all at once begin singing a tone. If you are doing it correctly, you should get a little popping sound as the tone begins. This is called a glottal attack.

Starting a tone with a glottal attack can help establish the coordination that seals the cords and keeps them from allowing this extra air to escape. Simply practice this exercise by repeating a glottal attack on a single note three times on the vowel "ah." Then modulate up by half steps throughout your entire range.

Figure 6.1. Glottal Exercise

Remember, the goal for both the singer who is unable to produce a breathy quality and the singer who only sings with a breathy tone is not to lose their current stylistic approach, but rather to expand their stylistic tool kit. When it comes to style, you should have your cake and eat it too.

Adding a Little "Stank"

By adding some tension in the throat, it is possible to sing with a little rasp, gravel, grit, or stank (as I call it) in your tone. Many modern singers use this technique. While most vocal coaches would call my next statement heresy, I believe there is a place for this in modern style, and I believe it can be done without detriment to the vocal health of the singer.

The key is that when using this technique the singer must be careful not to sing too loudly or to use this sound too consistently. Think of this stylistic tool as salt for the stew—use it sparingly. If you take the lid off the jar and dump all the salt into the stew, and you sing with this tone all the time, you've ruined the stew and could be at risk of ruining your voice. The majority of the singing that you do must be effortless, open, and free from tension. With that as the foundation for your overall sound and stylistic approach, this technique, when used for the occasional accent or ornament, and performed at moderate volume levels (let the mic do the work!), can be part of a lifetime of healthy singing without any setbacks or compromises in vocal health. And it sounds cool, so go for it—with caution!

For a demonstration of the effects of using different tone colors, check out the video demonstration on the DVD-ROM:

Video Example 6.2. Style Demo: Tone Color

Vibrato

The goal for vibrato use varies greatly from style to style. In classical styles the goal is to have a consistent vibrato that is heard on every sustained note. In vocal jazz ensembles like the Manhattan Transfer, vibrato is rarely used, especially when singing harmonies. In musical theater you hear singers transition between straight tone and vibrato, sometimes even while sustaining the same pitch.

The important thing for the modern worship singer is to be able to control vibrato. There will be songs that require vibrato, and others that require more straight tone and control. You may even use vibrato differently in different sections of the same song. And if you want to be able to transition between stylistic genres and sound like you belong in the style you are singing in, the ability to control vibrato will be an important tool for you to possess. The ability to control vibrato can be challenging and elusive for many singers, and the nature of the challenge depends on what aspect of vibrato control they are struggling with.

I've worked with singers who have no vibrato, ever, and for them, the challenge is in simply bringing vibrato into the voice. They often feel that vibrato is a mysteriously elusive sound that they have no idea how to produce. I've also worked with singers who use lots of vibrato, and they wish they could give some of their vibrato to the singers without any.

We will explore how to develop vibrato control for each of these singers, but before we do, let's take a look at what vibrato is and what happens in the structure and function of the voice in order to produce it.

What Is Vibrato?

Merriam-Webster's dictionary says that vibrato is "a slightly tremulous effect imparted to vocal or instrumental tone for added warmth and expressiveness by slight and rapid variations in pitch." This is exactly right, but how does this tremulous effect—slight and rapid variation in pitch—happen?

When a consistent flow of energy is moving through our muscles, they shake. This is true for all of our muscles. If you picked up the heaviest rock that you could hold in one hand and held it with your arm stretched out, what would happen after just a few seconds? Your arm would begin to shake, right? What if you traveled to my friend's home in Iceland on New Year's Eve and stood outside to watch the fireworks go off at midnight, wearing exactly what you had on at the Fourth of July picnic in the States last summer? First of all of your muscles would tighten, you'd wrap your arms around your body to try and stay warm, and then you'd begin to shake. This is how muscles work.

Well, the same is true for the muscles that control the function of the larynx. When you hold a note, a consistent flow of energy moves through the muscles in your larynx in order to sustain that pitch. As that flow of energy continues moving through your larynx, the muscles begin to shake. The larynx actually oscillates up and down in your throat with very slight and rapid movement. This movement in the larynx changes the pitch. As the structure of the larynx moves up and down, so does the pitch you are holding.

In this diagram the straight line represents a sustained pitch. The wavy line moving through it represents the vibrato as it very rapidly adjusts the pitch slightly higher than the sustained note, and then slightly lower, and so on.

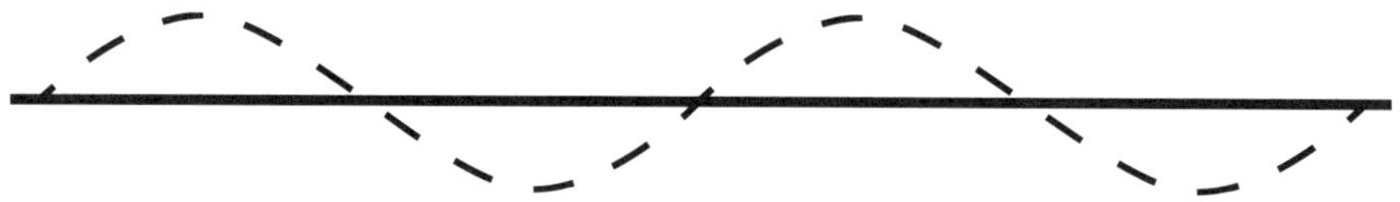

Figure 6.2. Oscillation of Vibrato

Developing the Vibrato

For the singer who comes in unable to produce vibrato, we begin to develop it through the principles of vocal freedom that we discussed earlier. Vibrato is a natural by-product of a relaxed, energized, and healthy vocal production. If there is no vibrato, most likely there is tension in the voice that is keeping the larynx locked in the throat, unable to shake up and down and create the vibrato.

Typically, as the singer focuses on eliminating tension from the voice, the vibrato will emerge without any thought. It just happens; one day the singer will be in a session, going through some exercises or singing a song, and I will say, "Hey, did you hear the vibrato come through on that pitch?"

Occasionally, though, the singer will be making fantastic progress in the effort to eliminate vocal tension, yet the vibrato is still elusive. In these cases, I recommend singing on a daily basis with some recordings of singers who use vibrato. For women I recommend the movie soundtrack from *The Sound of Music* with Julie Andrews. For men, any of Josh

Groban's CDs usually work nicely. I find that the singers who just have a good time and dance around the house singing, "The hills are alive . . ." usually make faster progress than the ones who take the pursuit quite seriously. Have some fun, and be silly, because for most singers who have never sung with vibrato, it *feels* silly when they first hear themselves producing vibrato. Some have even described it as fake—it doesn't feel like their voice. It doesn't feel like your voice because it's new and unfamiliar. Just go with it! The more you do it, the more natural it will become.

Controlling the Vibrato

Singers who have difficulty eliminating the vibrato are often coming from operatic training, classical musical theater, or a choral background that encourages the use of vibrato. All of these singers do the majority of their singing in an acoustic environment, meaning that they aren't singing into a microphone or using amplification. Their first step toward developing vibrato control is often simply to sing in a modern style at lower decibel levels. In other words, don't sing so loud!

Since vibrato emerges as a result of a movement of the larynx that is generated by the shaking of the muscles responsible for sustaining a pitch, the louder you sing, the more energy will be flowing through the muscles, and the more the larynx (and pitch) will oscillate. Often, all I have to do is put a microphone into a singer's hand, tell him or her to not project so much or sing with such force, fullness, and volume, and voilà, he or she is suddenly able to control the vibrato. Others may require a little more intentionality to reprogram their muscle memory.

A simple exercise can help. Begin singing a repeated phrase on a single pitch. It can be any phrase, but I believe in the power of positive thinking, so let's use "I can sing straight tone." Start off singing on a comfortable pitch and at a moderate volume. The first time through, sing each word on that pitch without too much sustain, fairly short and quick. Then repeat the phrase on the same pitch, this time sustaining the notes a little longer, all the while focusing on not allowing the vibrato to emerge, just like you did on the shorter phrase. Then, finally, sing the phrase on the same pitch again, this time holding each note for at least a few seconds, again focusing on not allowing the vibrato to emerge. It's a simple exercise, but I've seen it work well for hundreds of singers looking to establish the muscle memory of what it feels like to hold a sustained note without vibrato.

Tremolo

While vibrato is a natural oscillation in pitch, there is another vocal production called a tremolo that is an interruption in pitch. It often serves as an impostor for vibrato, especially for the singer challenged to sing with vibrato. Rather than a relaxed wave, the tremolo is a rapid pulsing that actually starts and stops the voice. If you can think of the way Elmer Fudd and Woody Woodpecker laugh, this is the same vocal effect as the tremolo. The singer often feels an aggressive, forced vocal approach rather than a relaxed, effortless production. Any of the tension areas can contribute to a tremolo, and discovering the feeling and coordination of the voice releasing will help eliminate it and allow the singer to find a natural vibrato.

Tongue Tension and Vibrato

One area of tension in particular that can influence the natural function of the vibrato is tongue tension. As we discussed on the chapter on vocal freedom, tongue tension is tension in which the hyoid bone at the base of the tongue pulls back and forces down against the top of the thyroid cartilage in the larynx. When the vibrato begins, it moves the tongue up and down along with the oscillation of the vibrato. You've probably seen singers who have a slight quiver to their bottom lip when they are holding out a note. This is a result of extreme tongue tension, and as the tongue moves up and down, it is so locked that the neighboring jaw muscles move right along with it. I've actually heard from colleagues of mine about singers they have encountered whose entire heads would shake up and down along with the vibrato. This causes significant problems in the function of the larynx, and also creates some interesting visual dynamics that can become a barrier to effective stage communication.

The good thing about this problem is that it is easily identified in the mirror. To free the voice from this tension, the tongue tension exercises outlined in the chapter on vocal freedom will need to be a daily part of your vocal workout. While the quiver may seem like an extreme vocal response to tension, it is easily remedied with consistent exercise and a reprogramming of the muscle memory.

Using Vibrato

Vibrato is a powerful tool, and its presence or absence significantly affects what is being communicated by the singer, and what is being experienced by the listener. Vibrato used at high volume levels can create a sense of strength and emphasis, while vibrato used on a soft pitch can create warmth and a depth of texture in the tone that allows listeners to "sink into" what they are hearing. A straight tone on a loud pitch can create a driving edge and a sense of unresolved tension, while a straight tone on a soft pitch can give a sense of innocence or intimacy that can be disarming to the listener.

Listen to how differently the last phrase of this song is experienced when it is sung first with vibrato, and then without.

Video Example 6.3. Style Demo: Vibrato

Same words, same notes, and yet a completely different emotion that is expressed by the singer and experienced by the listener as a result of the vibrato.

Here are a few other songs I recommend downloading and listening to:

- Rachael Lampa: "My Father's Heart"
- Linda Eder: "I Don't Know How to Say Goodbye"
- Phillips, Craig and Dean: "Your Grace Still Amazes Me"

It can often be helpful to use notation in our music in order to be intentional about our use of vibrato. Here is a simple system of notation that you can use:

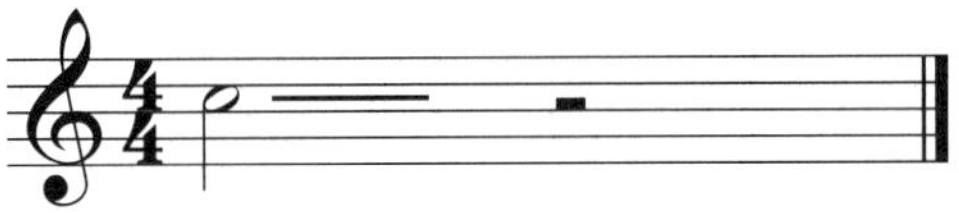

Figure 6.3. Notation for Straight Tone

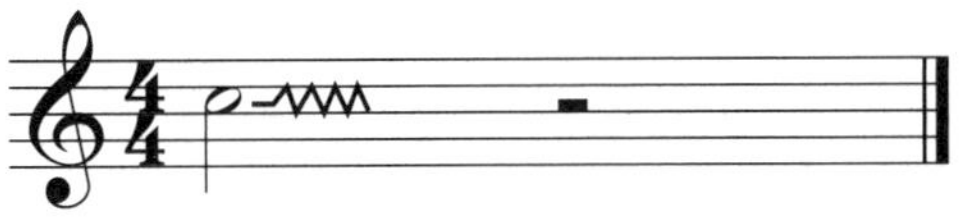

Figure 6.4. Notation for Vibrato

Pitch Adjustments

Pitch adjustments can come in a variety of forms. We can fall off of a pitch, we can bend into a pitch, or we can change up a melody with ornamentation. All three are important aspects of style that we need to develop and be able to control. We'll talk about the uniqueness of each and the colors that they can provide for our stylistic palette.

Pitch Bends

There are three ways that we can perform what is called the *attack* of a pitch, meaning how we approach the very beginning of singing a note. In classical or choral style the goal is to approach the pitch spot on. You don't begin above it or below it; you sing the exact pitch.

In jazz style, singers often approach the beginning of the pitch with a *scoop*. A scoop is a slow approach to the note you are going to sing that comes from underneath the tone. The distance from where you begin a scoop to the actual pitch you are going to sing can be a fairly substantial distance in some styles, even as much as a few semitones.

In modern worship style, we occasionally approach a note with a *pitch bend* or *hook*. A pitch bend doesn't cover as much distance as a scoop and is quicker to reach the destination note.

Listen to the samples on the CD demonstrating the differences between a pitch bend, a scoop, and the precise approach used in classical and choral styles.

Video Example 6.4. Style Demo: Pitch Bends

What a huge difference there is in these approaches. We can see the significance of this single stylistic tool and its effect on what we hear. Imagine having three people on a worship team with no control over their use of this tool. One of them has a precise approach, one of them scoops, and one of them consistently uses a modern pitch bend. On the worship team the singer using the pitch bends would be a good fit, but if you put all three of them together on the same team—that would be a mess! It doesn't matter how great their individual voices are, how developed their technique, how expansive their range; it's just a mess until they develop the ability to sing with a pitch bend to accent their style.

The best way to develop this ability is first to be consciously aware of it, and then to simply practice it. Pitch bend is not a difficult thing to control; it is more of a mental exercise. You have to pay attention, recognize when and how you are using it, and learn to be intentional and in control. The longer you've been using a scoop or a direct approach, the more challenging it will be to integrate a pitch bend into the style, because as soon as your mind checks out, familiar muscle memory will come back in and the old approach will return.

The best way to learn where and when to place a pitch bend in a modern worship song is to listen to professionals in the modern worship style and imitate them. Your ear will begin to learn the pattern and the places where pitch bends are most appropriate, and your voice will develop the coordination to implement this stylistic tool. We'll discuss how to listen to songs analytically at the end of this chapter.

Here is the notation we use in music to mark a pitch bend.

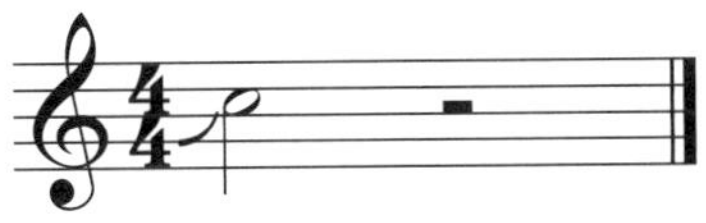

Figure 6.5. Notation for Pitch Bend

Fall-offs

A fall-off comes at the end of a note when the singer drops the pitch down, rather than stopping the note without changing the pitch at the end. It is a stylistic tool used occasionally in modern worship, but it should be used sparingly, as demonstrated by the singers you'll analyze in the exercise at the end of this chapter.

Here is the notation we use in music to mark a fall-off.

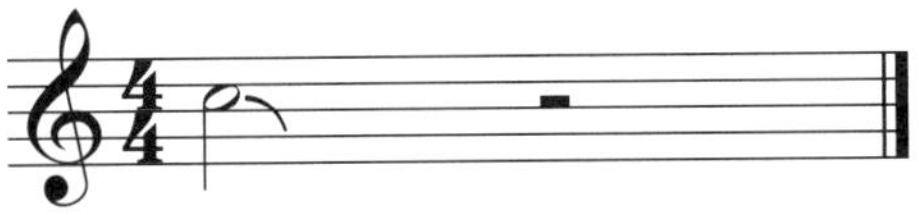

Figure 6.6. Notation for Fall-off

Ornamentation

Ornamentation (also called an ad-lib, improvisation, or riff) is when a singer deviates from the original melody line and sings alternate pitches, usually based on a blues scale. It's the *American Idol* "Why sing one note when you could sing seven?" approach to melody. In modern worship style it is rarely used in the context of an ensemble (or worship team) setting, but worship leaders (and sometimes a designated singer from the worship team) can often be heard using this stylistic tool as a lead-in to an upcoming phrase in the song, or toward the end of the song over the top of the chorus that the rest of the worship team and congregation are singing.

The singers I have worked with who did this the best developed the ability by listening and learning from what they heard other singers do. The genres that use this stylistic technique the most are gospel and R&B.

I would recommend the following CDs as a great resource for developing your ear to hear melodic ornamentation:

- For women: *The Preacher's Wife*, Whitney Houston
- For men: *Babyface*, The Day

These are two brilliant albums that provide opportunities throughout to sing along and develop your ear and vocal muscle memory to begin experimenting with this stylistic tool.

Stylistic Analysis

Now that we have broken down modern vocal style into four manageable tools, the next step is to develop our ability to control these stylistic tools and to integrate them into our singing. There are four steps to this part of the process.

1. Choose an Artist to Emulate

First, choose an artist who is singing in a style that you like. Choose your favorite song, making sure that it is in a realistic range for your voice and will not require you to concentrate too much on technique just in order to pull off the notes. You want to be able to focus completely on style. Make sure you have a recording of the original artist singing the song (and not someone "covering" the song), and then find a background track (that is, one without vocals—a karaoke track) that you can sing along with. Then print out the music to the song, or a lyric sheet of the entire song in a large font with some space between lines. Now you're ready to get to work.

2. Analyze Style

Next, listen through the song a few hundred times (well, at least a few dozen), analyzing every aspect of style one at a time. Take your lyric sheet and go through every phrase of the song, listening over and over to every sustained note to see if the artist uses vibrato or straight tone or transitions between the two. As you listen to each sustained note, mark your observations in your music or on your lyric sheet so that by the end, you have every use of vibrato or straight tone notated for the entire song. Now do the same thing for pitch bends, fall-offs, ornamentation. For vibrato, pitch bends, and fall-offs, use the notation introduced in this chapter.

For diction, write out the phonetics of any pronunciation that you will need to be conscious of. For tone color, try highlighting words with different colors. Maybe yellow for a pure tone, green for a breathy tone, and red for a tone with some gravel and stank in it. For ornamentation you can write the exact notes and rhythm the artist uses on the staff if you have the music; otherwise you can draw a line that generally maps out the contour of the ornamentation, going up as the pitch goes higher and drawing the line down as it gets lower.

By this point you've listened to the song enough to have a very multicolored, marked-up lyric sheet or piece of music.

3. Emulate Style and Record

The next step is to practice singing the song with the exact stylistic approach the original artist used. If the original artist used vibrato on a sustained note, you use vibrato on that sustained note. If the original artist used a breathy tone on a couple of notes and then transitioned back to a pure tone, your goal is to do the same. I call this a "vocalprint." Just like a fingerprint, you want to make an exact match of what the original artist performed.

Once you feel you have locked this in, then you are ready to record yourself singing the song, capturing your vocalprint.

4. Compare

The final step in the process involves putting your recording side by side with the original artist's recording and comparing how closely you emulated his or her style. You'll hear things that you thought worked that actually didn't, and you'll be surprised to hear areas that you thought may not have sounded or felt right, that captured the original artist's style. After you've completed this step, your work has just begun. Go back to the drawing board and begin the process again, applying the things you learned the first time around and increasing your stylistic control with each pass. Once you feel you have exhausted the stylistic development you can achieve from working with this song or artist, move on to a new song or artist who also demonstrates a stylistic approach that you would like to implement into your own singing.

Some singers I work with bristle at the thought of being a copycat of other artists. They have no interest in being the next (fill in the name of your favorite artist here). They want to be the first them, and develop their own unique stylistic approach, not mimic what someone else has already done. I respect that and support that wholeheartedly. However, all the great singers have been influenced by the great singers who came before them, and have developed their unique style not from a blank page, but from a full box of stylistic tools that they learned from other performers. This exercise will not leave you stuck in a stylistic rut; rather, as you add the stylistic tools you pick up from other singers to your own toolbox, you will be able to truly develop your own style with a full supply of tools and complete control.

Style to Express Your Heart in Worship

When you read the book of Psalms, David's conversations with God were hardly monotonous. David brought all of himself to worship, opening his heart fully and authentically to God. If we desire to express this full spectrum of response to God through our voices, we need all of the colors and options available to us. We need voices that capture and express what our hearts desire to convey. Style is not a box for you to fit into, nor is it an external requirement dictating what you can or can't do with your voice. Style provides you with new shades and colors on your ever-increasing vocal palette. So grab the brush and start painting!

7

Microphones and Monitors

In modern worship we live in an electronic world of amps and speakers and microphones. These developments in technology are a big part of what has allowed this genre of music to evolve, and they open up great possibilities to us as musicians in terms of what we are capable of doing. But to be successful singers in this environment, we need at least a basic understanding of the technology we use, how it works, and how we can use it to serve us best.

How a Microphone Works

As a singer in modern worship, you are completely dependent on the microphone in order to be heard. The microphone is part of the instrument you play; it is an extension of your voice, and so it is critical that you know how to use it. If you are singing modern worship on the stage of a church, there is a good chance you are holding in your hand a cardioid dynamic microphone. It's not important to our conversation to unpack all of what that means, but it is important to highlight what it means for you. A cardioid dynamic microphone is designed to pick up sound only from the direction that the head of the microphone is facing, and to pick up and highlight only the most prominent sound coming into the mic.

Proximity

There is a proximity effect involved with these microphones in that the closer the sound source gets to the mic, the "better" the sound becomes because the mic is able to augment more of the quality of the tone coming in. The reason for this is that we sing in an amplified environment, often competing with a lot of stage volume. These mics are designed to pick up sound from the closest source (your voice) so that you don't get that Fender amp that's blaring over 100 decibels of sound coming through the vocal mic as strongly as your voice.

Because these mics are built to enhance whatever sound is coming from the closest (and strongest) source, your voice will sound better the closer you hold the microphone to your mouth. Try an experiment with the mic you use on Sunday morning. Hold the microphone about an inch or two from your mouth and just speak. It doesn't matter what you say. Maybe try reciting the Gettysburg Address if you know it, or the 23rd Psalm, or your shopping list. Notice the tone as you speak. Your voice is projected, to be sure, but the tone is rather flat. Not much high end and not much low end. Now, without changing volume or emphasis, bring the mic right up to your bottom lip so that it is actually touching. Now repeat the same thing you just said into the mic. What a difference, right? The tone has more depth and richness (low end) and also more brightness and clarity (high end).

Check out the video demonstrating how to use a microphone on the DVD-ROM:

Video Example 7.1. Microphone Technique

If you hold the microphone this close to your mouth, the microphone will enhance the sound and send a signal that will make your voice sound better than it actually is. I don't care how good you are, that's always a good place to start! Once you have the mic that close, keep it there. Nothing drives a skilled sound engineer crazier than singers who are always moving the mic around and changing its position. Even one inch can have a dramatic effect on the signal being sent from the microphone to the soundboard. Bring the mic right up to your lips, so that most of the time you can feel it brushing your bottom lip as you sing, and don't move it, even on those loud high notes. We see this all the time from some of the best singers in the world. They pull the mic back when they are about to increase their volume or jump to that higher note, and it looks kind of cool—except to the sound engineer. What this does is take all of the control out of your engineer's hands. The reason that singers have learned to do this is that many of them started their careers singing in venues with their band where they had to set up their own equipment and didn't have the budget for a sound person to run the board during the performance or service. The levels would get set, and away they'd go. In that setting, singers have to "ride the faders" and control their own volume with the proximity of the mic. If you have a skilled sound engineer back on the board, don't do this! Keep the mic close without exception in order to send the best signal to the board. Some churches, however, have very well-intentioned sound engineers who don't have a lot of expertise beyond getting everything turned on and functional. If this is the case, and you find (or you hear from a trusted person in the auditorium who's listening to your voice) that every time you are really singing out the sound gets distorted and "blown out," you may have to revert to the technique of pulling the mic away when your volume peaks.

Holding the Mic

Holding the microphone close to your mouth is the first step, and an important one. The positioning of the mic is also important. You don't want to hold the mic at a right angle to your face. This will hide much of your face, which will take away the best tool you have for communication. At a right angle you are also at greater risk of having your consonants pop like a percussion instrument when you strongly articulate your words. The reason for this is that the diaphragm of the mic is stretched flat across the face of the microphone, just behind the windscreen (the rounded, dome-shaped end that you sing into). When the breath that is expelled from a crisp consonant hits the diaphragm head-on it creates a popping sound as the breath abruptly pushes into it.

Hold the head of the microphone right at your bottom lip, but position the mic so that your hand is down by your chin and the mic is extended up toward your mouth at an angle, just like you're about to take a lick from the top of an ice cream cone. This will allow the percussive consonants to pass over the top of the diaphragm, but because of the proximity (keep the mic touching your bottom lip!) you will still get all of the benefits that the mic has to offer.

Choosing a Mic

For most singers in a worship setting at a church, you're pretty much stuck using whatever mic gets handed to you in sound check. If you have the chance to do any choosing, either for your own use or in a worship setting, the most popular stage microphone for singers is a Shure SM58. It's very popular because it sounds great and is affordable and amazingly durable (if you can't find your hammer and need to hang up pictures in your studio, you can use your SM58 to knock the nails into the wall, and the mic will most likely be fine for years to come).

I have seen more and more churches using Sennheiser brand mics as well, and the e835 seems to be the most popular choice.

Both of these mics are affordable, offer great quality, and get my vote for the best entry-level stage mics for vocalists on the market.

Monitor Systems

In the amplified world we sing in for modern worship, we are completely dependent on the microphone to be heard, and we are completely dependent on monitors in order to hear. For most worship singers in a church, hearing themselves is a constant issue and the source of a lot of frustration. However, there is hope! A basic understanding of monitor systems and how they work, a few tips, and some minor adjustments can go a long way in helping singers to get what they need from their monitor mix.

Floor Monitors

When I first started singing worship in church over 20 years ago, the sound world was ruled by floor monitors. Floor monitors are black, angled boxes with speakers in them that sit on the stage and point up toward the musicians who need to hear them. Usually floor monitors are set up so that you can have different mixes on the stage. For example, the guitar player may only want to hear bass, drums, and the primary worship leader in his or her monitor, but the worship leader prefers to hear only the keyboard, guitar, and other singers. Floor monitors allow the sound engineer to designate different monitors for different people on stage, giving them their own unique mix.

The biggest problem with floor monitors is that they are loud. In the amplified environment of modern worship, before we even turn on a floor monitor, we already have a lot of noise on the stage. The drum set makes a ton of racket, and then many of your instrumentalists are going to be generating their own sound from their amps. Add a percussionist, brass section, or worship choir to the mix, and we're already starting sound check with a lot of volume on the stage. Then we add a floor monitor for each instrument on stage, and sometimes multiple vocal monitors depending on the number of singers, and the volume on stage increases. This can make it difficult for anyone on stage to hear anything, and it can also drastically reduce the quality of sound in the auditorium, as much of what is heard is coming through stage monitors rather than the main house speakers.

In-Ear Monitors

In-ear monitors function in much the same way as floor monitors, only instead of sitting on the floor and creating stage volume, they are inserted into your ear. In-ear monitors come standard with buds that you place in your ear, or you can pay to have plastic molds created to the exact shape of the inside of your ear. The great benefit with in-ear monitors is that they create no stage volume and they put exactly what you need to hear directly into your ear. Many of them (especially the individually molded inserts) even serve to seal out stage volume.

In-ear monitors also give the singer greater control, independent of the assistance of the sound engineer. Many systems are set up with wireless packs that allow the singer to pan between two sound options (usually instrumentals on one channel and vocals on another, or the singer's own vocals on one channel and a balanced mix of everything else on the other). Some systems (such as the Aviom monitor systems) even provide your own little "mixing board" on stage, allowing you to adjust the level of every instrument and singer in the mix you hear in their monitors.

A very important consideration with in-ear monitors is to make sure that you are protecting your ear against potential damage from high volumes. Because the source of the sound is so close to your eardrum, your ear is at risk of being damaged. Just be conscious of this, and conservative in the amount of volume you allow in your mix, and you should be fine. If you ever find that your ears are ringing after a service, have a conversation with your sound engineer or worship leader and make some adjustments so that you don't end up going for months with a dangerous level of volume being piped into your monitors.

What Is Essential?

Many singers get frustrated with monitors because their expectations aren't realistic. The singer who has only heard his or her favorite iTunes playlist through headphones or speakers and is expecting something similar to come through the monitor system will always be disappointed. The goal is not Dolby Surround Sound that will give you goose bumps at how fabulous you sound. The goal is functionality; that's it. If you can hear a rhythm center to keep you in tempo, a harmonic center to keep you in tune, and enough of your own voice to keep you from getting off from either of those, you should consider it a lucky day on stage leading worship—that's all you really need.

If you're using floor monitors, there's probably a pretty low-end speaker in that black box, and you could pipe tracks of the best musicians in the world, mixed by a top engineer, and it still wouldn't sound that great. There just isn't time to get you an amazing mix—nor do you really need one. Lower your standards and focus on the essentials—rhythm, pitch, and enough of your voice that you can tell when you're off.

A friend in the music industry told me about a conversation he'd had with a Grammy-winning artist who has toured every inhabitable continent on the globe, singing to sold-out stadiums of tens of thousands of people. The budget for this artist's tours is virtually limitless, affording him the best technology and crew that money can buy. On tour, he had at least one person dedicated completely and entirely to running monitors. There was a separate mixing board backstage dedicated exclusively to the monitor mix. The engineer running the board was always one of the best audio engineers in the world. My friend asked this artist how often his monitor mix was what he wanted. The answer: never, not once. If those resources don't provide a singer with the mix he or she desires, it's safe to assume that as a singer in a church, you're never going to like your mix, and the sooner we can get over that, the sooner we can focus on getting the mix we need that will allow us to sing at our best.

Singing from Muscle Memory

Since you know you're not really going to hear yourself the way you want to, and some days will be even worse than others, it is important to understand that your ears cannot dictate how much volume you use when you sing. Over-singing is one of the worship vocalist's greatest nemeses. When you over-sing and push your voice beyond what it is capable of, it sends your vocal quality down the drain, you lose vocal control and pitch accuracy, and you are practicing one of the quickest ways to blow out your voice and potentially cause damage.

There will come a time when you absolutely cannot hear yourself in the monitor mix at all. The temptation is to sing louder so that you can push your voice over the top of all of the stage volume. Go up against a guitar amp and you will lose that battle every time.

What we have to rely on in those situations is muscle memory, the feel of singing properly. You are getting into the vocal gym 20–30 minutes, three to four times per week for a reason. As you discover freedom, control, and range for your voice, and a production that is characterized by effortless singing, use your practice time to memorize that feeling. You will need to sing from that place in order to sound your best. Just like a pilot flying on instruments in a dense fog with no visibility, sing from muscle memory and "feel" when you're not able to hear yourself on stage. It will produce the best sound (even though you might not hear it) and it will protect your voice from damage.

The Volume Battle

When dealing in the world of floor monitors, none of us can hear ourselves on stage the way we need to. So here is what usually happens. The bass player asks for a little more of himself and the electric guitar in the monitor. Well, that drives up the overall stage volume and now the acoustic guitar player staged next to him can't hear herself, so she asks for a little more of her guitar in the monitor and a little more of the worship leader's vocals. Now the worship team that is sharing a monitor staged right in front of those two can't hear their own voices, and so they ask for more of themselves. As soon as one vocalist is brought up in that shared monitor, the other vocalists can't really hear themselves, so they ask for a little more, which then throws off the mix for everyone else, and the volume battle escalates, getting louder and louder.

A great way to think about what you need in your monitor is to focus on what you don't need, and ask for things to be brought down and taken out, especially when you're using floor monitors. Reducing or eliminating what you don't need allows what you do need to hear to pop out, and in the process the overall stage volume goes down, which helps everyone.

Stage Setup

Another tip that will help you get the monitor mix you need is to make sure you're positioned well on the stage. If the singers are directly in front of the drums, or the brass section, or the electric guitar player's amp, it doesn't matter how hard you work to dial in the right mix, you're simply not going to hear yourself until you move to a different position on stage. Be sure to spend some time each week before rehearsing with the band to decide on a stage setup. If your tech team or worship leader does that on his or her own, offer to come in and help so that time and frustration can be saved prior to rehearsal.

Sound Check the Vocal Mics

A really productive thing we would do every week in sound check when I was on staff at Willow Creek Community Church outside of Chicago was to check the vocal monitor mix separate from the band. We would do a quick general sound check on each vocalist, and then have all the vocalists sing a cappella together on one of the choruses from a song in the set for that service. We would begin with everyone singing with a lot of volume and energy, followed by the same section sung softly and tenderly. Then we'd give each singer the chance to offer some feedback on how he or she liked the mix, and we'd make some adjustments until we had everything locked in and everyone comfortable with the vocal mix, even the band. This would typically take approximately five minutes. This made life a lot easier once the band started playing, since we had started with a vocal mix that got everyone what they needed. All we had to focus on after that was balancing the band with that overall vocal mix, saving valuable rehearsal time.

Communicating with Your Sound Engineer

Your sound engineer should be your best friend, someone you treat like royalty. You should know what that person's favorite drink is at Starbucks and deliver one, accompanied by a dozen Krispy Kreme donuts (hot ones!) every time you show up for Sunday morning sound check. Everything you do goes through the sound engineer, and he or she has the power to either make you or break you.

Too often in a worship setting I have observed singers act like spoiled prima donnas and disrespect the sound engineers, treating them like second-class citizens who are there to serve them and just can't ever get it right. We'll talk more about an aspect of this in the chapter on the characteristics of a worship vocalist, but for now, here are a couple of tips that will go a long way in building bridges between the stage and the booth.

Life in the Booth

On more than one occasion I have taken a singer out of the worship-leading rotation who was copping an attitude with our sound engineers, and assigned him or her to be the assistant to the monitor engineer the next Sunday morning. I give the sound engineer instructions to provide the singer with some day-of training and then, as much as possible, to sit back and let the singer control the monitor mix for the morning. It's amazing how differently that singer shows up to sound check the next week he or she is scheduled on the team. The experience of understanding the number of dials and buttons that are involved in fulfilling each request that comes from the stage goes a long way in shaping a performer's perspective. Running a monitor mix and keeping a stage full of artists happy is challenging work. Even without the attitude issues I've mentioned, I think it's good for every singer to have a basic knowledge of how to run a sound board and mix monitors, so they can develop a vocabulary and an understanding of what is going on for the person they are communicating with. Sound engineers want to help you; that's a big part of what they are there for. Always show respect and learn to communicate in a way that will help them to help you.

Listen and Communicate Intelligently

One of the simplest ways we can do this is to listen before we speak. Singers who get frustrated in a sound check or rehearsal and just blurt out, "I can't hear!" don't do anything but raise the blood pressure of everyone around them. Before you ask for an adjustment, ask yourself what you are hearing in your monitor. What are you needing to hear that you don't? What are you hearing too much of that needs to be brought down? Is there anything that you can get rid of? Remember, start with what you don't need and bring your mix down, rather than boosting what you think you need to hear more.

Workshop

Ask your sound engineer if he or she would be willing to lead a two-hour workshop on a Saturday morning to educate the singers on the team about the technology being used. It's a great opportunity for the engineer to communicate once, to everyone, things that each singer needs to know. You can establish some new systems that will help streamline your process, and provide a laboratory for singers to go through a sample sound check with time to experiment and learn, without the pressure of a service bearing down on them.

8

Stage Presence and Communication

As I mentioned in the introduction, the overarching theme of all of the work I do with my clients is to help them unleash their hearts through song. Vocal technique is critical if we hope to find the ability in our voices to express what our hearts long to convey through our music. But it is equally critical that we develop the ability to connect our hearts to our physical expression in order to lead worship with an authenticity and vulnerability that are contagious and engaging.

I have experienced singers with amazing vocal ability—the kinds of voices that can blow you through the back wall with their power and range, or take your breath away with their control and style. And yet many of these singers are limited in their effectiveness by aspects of their stage presence and communication. Without knowing it they create barriers and obstacles with the way they use hand gestures, facial expression, and many other elements of stage presence. And in worship, the number of pitfalls only increases because of the unique dynamics of this environment. Worship singers can't rely on simply performing to get by. Effective communication for worship reveals a genuine and transparent heart—an experience that can touch people's souls, change lives, and create moments where it feels as though heaven is touching earth.

And yet some of the worst communication skills can be found on the stages of churches all over the world every weekend. Singers with great hearts, motivation, and even vocal talent are not as effective as they could be because of aspects of their stage presence. The good news for these singers is that there are simple, practical tools that any singer can learn and develop to physically express the heart's inspiration.

Know What You're Singing About

The first step in effective stage communication for worship is to simply know what you're singing about. I'm not talking about memorizing the words. Over the years as I've coached vocalists, I've been amazed at how many times, in the final stages of the rehearsal process, singers have been unable to tell me what a song is about. They can recite all the words, they can sing every note, but they can't explain in two or three sentences of their own words what the song is about, or how the song has spoken to them. If we're honest, we've all probably been there before. The weekly demand to crank out another service can be intense. Sometimes we feel as if simply remembering the song and not messing up is about as much as we can pull off. But if you don't take the time to become intimately familiar with the message of the song, then you can't connect your heart with the music you plan to sing. Our worship becomes a sing-along time where we are simply regurgitating memorized lyrics and melody. The potential is far greater! We can open our hearts, communicate from our soul to the God of the Universe, and, by modeling that, invite others to do the same. That's pretty amazing! But we can't hope to do that if we don't know what we're singing about. What is the song really saying? What message does it hold for us? What things come up for me as I shine the light of the song's message into the deepest parts of my soul? When we can answer those questions, then we know the song, and we are ready to lead others into their own response to the song.

Here are a couple of simple, practical steps you can take to get to know a song prior to singing it:

1. Read the words. This seems obvious, but it can be difficult to internalize the words of a song if you only read them while you're singing. Sit back, relax, and simply read through the lyrics, over and over again, asking God to open your ears to what the Spirit might be saying through the words of the song. Take the time to allow a single sentence to speak to you. Allow it to examine your life and illuminate what needs to be revealed and brought forward.

2. Take time to listen. Get a recording of the song and just listen—don't sing! Simply receive the song and listen to what it has to say to you. Don't multitask while you're doing it. Create space where you can be quiet and undistracted, where the only thing happening is you quieting your heart, opening your soul, and allowing the words of the song to penetrate you with its message.

Taking these first steps toward knowing the song launches you into the meaningful journey of connecting your story to the music you sing, the next step in the process of developing effective stage communication for worship.

Tell Your Story

Every one of us has a story, experiences and relationships that have become the script to our lives. Effective communication for worship requires that we allow the songs we sing to intersect with the story of our life. We reflect on how the words of a song speak to the current events of our life, or the condition of our heart. We ask ourselves if a song's message has implications for our relationships or the way we are experiencing God in our life.

And then we need to show up! We need to bring ourselves, and every part of ourselves, onto the stage and lead from an authentic place that comes from the very core of what is completely true for us and about us. But so many singers miss this opportunity because they assume some role or character as soon as they walk onto the stage to lead worship. They jump into their worship leader persona, they start using facial expressions and hand gestures that they never use in any other context, and they move their bodies and tap their feet, and do that thing where they slap the side of their leg with their hand—come on, you've seen it, and maybe you've even done it! It ends up becoming worship choreography. It reads as fake and artificial, and it has become (for many singers) a rote exercise that is safe and risk free, because it doesn't require that their hearts be even in the same building.

I am not saying that hand gestures and kinesthetic movement should be avoided, or that if you use those gestures you're a fake. What is critical is that every gesture, every movement and facial expression come from a place that is vitally connected to the meaning and communication of the song. You simply must bring yourself, your story, and your experiences onto the stage with you—all of who you are, all that has made you who you are, every good, bad, ugly, beautiful, and redeemed part that makes you uniquely you! We can't hope to be vitally connected in our worship leadership if we don't even show up. And, sadly, this is the case for most of the singers I experience in worship. Their focus is on remembering the words, or trying to remember whether they repeat the chorus or go to the bridge, or wondering what people in the congregation are thinking about them, or why Suzie got to lead the song again this week—on and on. Effective stage leadership for worship takes place only when all of those distractions slip away and all that remains is us, the song, and our God.

Showing up in that way is difficult, though. It's a lot easier to leave our hearts and our stories in the front row as we walk onto the stage and step into a worship performance. Assuming a role, behaving the way we think we are expected to act on stage while we lead worship, is safe, with no surprises. Bringing all of who we are to our worship gets messy. There's an emotional vulnerability that comes in when we bring our complete selves onto the stage. What if we don't want to bring all of ourselves onto the stage? What if there are parts of ourselves that we want to hide and not bring out into the light? What happens if the pot gets stirred while we're on the stage, and emotion comes up, and people get a view into what is really happening under the surface? That's scary! And powerful!

Think of the last time you were in a congregation of people being led in worship and you were deeply impacted by the experience. It could have happened in your home church, at a conference, or even at a concert in a large arena. What do you remember about the singers and worship leader? Was their leadership safe? Were they emotionally distant, with worship smiles pasted on their faces, moving their bodies and gesturing with pre-programmed motions? My guess is that the leadership you experienced was raw and vulnerable, not a cheap performance. My guess is that all the singers on that stage were completely embodying all of who they were, bringing that to all of who God is, and expressing the song from that level of depth, truth, and authenticity. And as a result you responded by engaging your heart in the same way. That is the place where worship leadership becomes effective, because God is in that. "Where two or three are gathered together in my name, there am I in the midst of them" (Matthew 18:20, KJV). But if we don't even show up, how do we expect that the Spirit of God will fill the place, stirring people's hearts and transforming lives?

When we show up, completely and authentically, not only do we become energy conductors for the Spirit of God, but we model for our congregation exactly what we are inviting them to experience and engage in. When the congregation sees authentic, vulnerable worship being led from the heart, the feeling becomes contagious—they want to worship in the same way. But when what they see is safe and performed, they will also be compelled to engage in the same way.

As I consult with worship teams across North America, I often hear these questions and comments from the worship leader: "What can we do to make our services more alive? Our congregation is so unresponsive!" "Should we pick better songs, or make them stand up and clap more often?" "Should we turn up the guitar in the house mix?" The list goes on and on. Igniting the fire in a congregation begins by modeling that passion from the stage. It is rarely an external knob that needs to be turned. It is a matter of the heart. We need to make sure that our hearts are so vitally connected to every word that comes out of our mouths that our stage leadership is authentic, passionate, and engaging.

When our congregations experience inauthentic stage leadership, they may not fully engage the way we desire, but what happens when people who are visiting from the outside experience worship performance? We've become accustomed to it in the Christian subculture. A non-Christian will sniff out anything that's artificial and fake from a mile away, and most likely that will be the end of it. They may not be sure what they are looking for, but they know that it is not that. Authentic stage communication is not only critical for engaging the hearts of our congregation, but it can also be the environment that draws someone who has drifted far away to draw close to the heart of God.

Bring It All Together

Effective worship leadership takes place at the intersection between these two values we have discussed:

1. Knowing what the song is about
2. Bringing all of who we are

But how do we do that as we prepare for Sunday morning? Let's take the lyrics from Chris Tomlin's song "Enough" as an example.

All of You is more than enough for all of me
For every thirst and every need
You satisfy me with Your love
And all I have in You is more than enough.

OK, this is a cool song with a catchy melody and a great, guitar-driven groove—it would be really easy to get up and sing it with your worship smile on, just movin' and groovin' on autopilot. But let's first take a step back and look at these lyrics as an opportunity for you to truly engage your heart in the communication of this song.

"All of You." What does that mean? All of who God is—wow! Take a moment to just sit with that. Who is God? What are the characteristics of God, the nature of God? You could spend a lifetime marveling at that awareness and still never capture the full reality of "All of You."

Now let's take a look at the next line, "Is more than enough for all of me." More than enough—there's a lot there, too! This song is saying that all of who God is, is more than enough—more! For all of me—all! Every part of who I am, everything that defines and has made me who I am, God is more than enough for all of that—all of it!

Every thirst, every need, God satisfies. With love—God's love! Sit with that for a moment. Consider God's love. Open your heart and your mind to the truth of what that means, of how big that is, and the fact that all that is good and right and true in the entire world is based on and flows out of God's love. This is another concept that we could sit with for eternity and never fully grasp.

And now listen. Listen to the song, over and over again, until you feel it penetrate your heart and seep into your soul. Maybe there will be some deep emotion that comes to the surface as you allow yourself to sink into the truth of this song and allow it to wash over you. Maybe thoughts and insight will flood your mind. Whatever comes is perfect. Just listen, and don't filter. Whatever comes, let it come.

Once we've sat with the song and allowed it to speak to us so that we have a knowledge and awareness of what the song is about, it's time to bring our lives, our stories, all of our experiences and relationships to the song we are going to sing. Here are some questions you might ask to begin the process of bringing all of who you are out of hiding and into the light of the truth of this song.

In what ways has God proven that He can satisfy your deepest desires? Have there been times when God provided for you in ways that filled your heart to overflowing? Are you acutely aware of the areas in your life where you are looking for other things to satisfy the needs and thirsts that only He can satisfy? Are there areas of your life where you are not allowing God to be enough, because you don't feel like you can even bring them to God—because they're in hiding?

By bringing your story to a song, you open yourself more fully to God's presence with you as you sing. You engage in an authentic conversation that connects your heart to the words of the song, and suddenly your communication comes to life.

One of the questions I often receive when working with someone in this area is "How do I deal with strong emotions when they surface while I am trying to sing?" Or, in other words, "How do I cry and sing at the same time?" My first response is, if that's your problem, God bless you for it! You're already two steps ahead of the game. What a gift to be so emotionally connected to singing that you need to be concerned with the effects of that emotion on your performance.

It is true that singing and crying are fairly mutually exclusive pursuits. I have found that if you tend to be overtaken with emotion while you are leading, or if a particular song happens to strike a chord in your heart, it can help to spend a lot of time crying through the song before the day comes to walk onstage and sing. I've known singers who needed a good two or three weeks to sit with a song, and allow all of the emotions to come up and pour out, before they were ready to step onstage and maintain enough composure to get through the performance. What happens through that process is beautiful, because rather than stuffing the emotions for the sake of duty, you are inviting your emotions to flow, to be seen and experienced fully. By the time Sunday morning rolls around, you'll be able to be authentic and feel into the song, but the emotions that come up will be expected, so you'll be able to maintain enough stability to be effective in your role as a singer.

I also feel that the occasional instance where emotion takes over, and tears come, even to the point where the singer is unable to sing, can be more than okay. It can be an amazing and beautiful moment where true emotion can be expressed and a congregation's heart can be opened and engaged. I would much rather experience worship where things occasionally get a little messy, than a safe, performed sing-along time.

Just Do It

This type of transformational communication takes only two steps, but it requires vulnerability and commitment. What's the alternative if we don't take the risk or invest the time? Communication can end up being about what we think we should be doing—with our hands, our body movements, our arms, and our facial expression. We try to bring "energy" to our worship, attempting to look engaged in order to draw people into the experience. But all of these motivations are externally focused, and what ends up being communicated is an artificial, disconnected performance. We want our congregation to see something real, something that draws them into what is happening, and something that motivates them to open their hearts to God in the same way they see we have.

So take the risk. Take the time. This Sunday, bring your story with you onto the stage. Allow your song to be an authentic dialogue between you and the God of the Universe. See the song as an opportunity to connect with God and allow Him to speak to you and through you. If you do, you create an opportunity for heaven to touch earth.

10 Common Pitfalls

1. **Repetitive Gestures**
   Watch out for those "go to" gestures that you use all the time. Repetition can become distracting, and overuse of the same gesture can take away its impact and effectiveness. It can, however, provide some additional entertainment for the youth who take part in our services as they count the number of times we use our signature "move."
2. **Repetitive Motion**
   Avoid consistent movement, like swaying, that can become a focus of our congregation and distract from the effectiveness of our leadership.
3. **No Service Review**
   In this day of digital media there is simply no excuse for not recording and reviewing your services. Most of us have a video camera that we carry around in our pocket on our phone, so the technology is there and available. It doesn't have to be anything fancy. Even a still shot of the stage, with a consumer-level video recorder set on a tripod, will allow us to see our stage leadership and recognize things we would have had no idea we were doing otherwise. It's a great exercise to do as a team. When I was at Willow Creek, all of the singers would meet in my office after the first service and we would watch the entire worship set. It is a painful experience, to be sure, but we always walked out with a keen awareness of what we were

doing that worked and came across as authentic and engaging, as well as what was distracting from the effectiveness of our leadership. Then, with that fresh in our minds, we had the opportunity to walk onto the stage in the very next service and make adjustments. It was like a built-in laboratory and system for development in this area. If you don't have enough time in between services to do this, consider having everyone meet during the sermon of the first service and use that time for your worship review. The pastor will be saying the same things in the next service, so you can still catch everything then.

4. **Lateral Movement**
   Be sure that any time you change your position on the stage, taking steps to the side, forward, or backward, you are intentional about that movement. Lateral movement is a strong communicator, and the important thing is to make sure that it is communicating what you want it to communicate, because whatever it is communicating, it is going to communicate it loudly. How can we know how lateral movement is being "read" in the house? Record yourself (see above), or ask a trusted friend or friends for their input.

5. **Clothing**
   As soon as the congregation has become focused on what we are wearing, our clothing has become a distraction. By all means, look good, be fashionable and relevant to the congregation you are serving with what you wear, but if you are making the right wardrobe choices, your congregation shouldn't even really notice what you are wearing. It's no fun for any worship leader to have to talk with a member of the team about revealing clothing. Err on the side of conservative, and consider sight lines. That skirt (or kilt, depending on what part of the world you live in) may be fine in the mirror at home, but is it long enough when you put it on a five-foot stage with seats directly under it?

6. **Closing Your Eyes**
   Closing your eyes can communicate a deep connection to what you are singing. It can also produce a wall between you and your congregation if you do it too much. Consistently closing your eyes can create the sense that you are having your own personal worship experience and the congregation is an outside observer. Your eyes are the window to your soul, and they

give the congregation an intimate view into your response to what you are singing about. Be sure that they are open often enough that your connection to the song can become contagious and inviting.

7. **Overly Animated Worship**

   Some singers use gestures that are larger than life, gestures they reserve for the stage. They come across as highly dramatic and can appear showy. I am not suggesting that we shouldn't be animated and kinesthetically involved when we lead worship, but we always need to have the "authenticity meter" up. We need to continually ask ourselves: Are our gestures coming from a place where we are so fully and passionately connected to what we are singing that we cannot help but communicate in precisely this way? If so, then our gestures are internally motivated.

   Are our gestures coming from a desire to look good, or a sense that "This is what effective worship leaders do—I know because I just went to a big worship concert that was in town last night," or because we always get really good feedback from people when we lead worship in this way? If so, then our gestures are externally motivated.

   The same gesture coming from a place of internal versus external motivation will read completely differently in the room. We need to make sure that everything we do flows out of a place of authenticity—connecting the heart to physical expression.

8. **No Communication**

   On the other side of the continuum, I see many singers leading worship, and supposedly they are passionate and connected to the message they are singing about. And yet they never move their bodies, and their faces are void of any emotion whatsoever.

   I lived in Chicago for 15 years. Through that entire time I stayed completely loyal to my hometown Seattle sports teams, but I did adopt the Chicago Cubs and now, after 20 years, consider myself a die-hard Cubs fan. The Cubs have not won the World Series in over 100 years, and when they do (oh, yes, it's going to happen!), Wrigleyville and the entire north side of Chicago will be total bedlam. Let's imagine that it's just minutes after the game has been won and a lifelong Cubs fan comes up to you and yells, "The Cubs won! The Cubs won!"—with an expressionless face and a motionless body. That's just weird, right? And yet that's exactly what happens for many singers every Sunday morning. They are supposedly wholeheartedly engaged in worship, and yet we see no outward physical signs of that emotional connection.

We have to be true to who we are, and I expect there to be some variation in communication from one singer to the next. We all have different personalities, different responses to a song, different stories that we bring onto the stage. That diversity is a beautiful thing, and it's important that the diversity that we find in our congregations also be represented on the stage. However, some of us need a little push out of our comfort zone, and we need to take some risks to allow the excitement and passion we feel in our hearts to come through in our physical expression. You know who you are!

9. **Mic Position**

   Facial expression accounts for the vast majority of our communication. If we position our microphone (either in a stand or while we hold it) at a right angle to our face, we cover our greatest communication tool. Hold the mic at a slight angle to your mouth, just as you would hold an ice cream cone right before you're going to lick it. You'll eliminate the percussion section that can materialize as you blast your consonants directly into the diaphragm of the mic, and you'll also let us see your face as you express authentic worship.

10. **Eye Contact with Congregation**

   There are certainly times when it is appropriate to make direct eye contact with people in the congregation. Even at those times, however, I usually suggest to singers that they look directly over the heads of the people in the back row of the main level. It eliminates the possibility of distraction for you and the congregation, and it will still give the congregation the sense that you are singing directly to them.

   It is inappropriate and distracting for us to be singing to the congregation when the song we sing is a message that is intended to be directly communicated to God. Singing "And I, I'm desperate for you. And I, I'm lost without you" into the eyes of a stranger—that's just weird and unnerving!

9

The "Inner Game" of Singing

The Importance of Your Internal World

I've been working with singers for over 20 years, and there is never a dull moment. Every person I've worked with is unique; however, many of them have certain tendencies in common. Singers are often very emotionally sensitive people. They wear their feelings on their sleeves and can be easily hurt if someone is insensitive to them. Singers often feel things deeply and passionately and walk through life significantly impacted by all that goes on around them. It causes challenges for singers, but it is also why they have the ability to grab a microphone and absolutely take the breath out of a room with a performance. It is part of the gift they give to the world. Others are able to feel and experience things through a song that they do not have the capacity to experience on their own.

The process of developing as a singer and reaching your full potential is never just about building technique. Every singer I have worked with has, to one degree or another, internal issues that limit his or her potential. Sometimes a singer's ability to fully develop his or her voice has more to do with overcoming those internal hang-ups than it has to do with building vocal technique.

Internal issues can absolutely stifle and paralyze a singer. On the flip side, I have seen singers boldly and courageously face those challenges and sing as they were never able to sing before. Sometimes such breakthroughs have very little to do with the technique that I've taught them, and everything to do with the internal work they do.

I tell people when they begin the process of vocal training, "This is going to be about more than just singing." It always looks different from one person to the next, and I can't predict exactly what will come up or how; I just know that for every singer, the ability to face internal barriers that hold back progress is an essential part of the journey toward becoming the best singer he or she can be.

In this chapter I will identify the most common issues I've seen and discuss their effects. We'll also take a look at some of the values that will help us to move beyond these limitations and to do the work we need to do to be free to sing at our best. Having seen hundreds of singers face their issues head-on and unleash their vocal potential as a result, I invite you to join them in that amazing journey.

Internal Issues That Influence Our Singing

Lack of Confidence

A client of mine named Diana said, "The main reason I wanted to take lessons was because of my confidence level. I have conversations in my head where I tell myself that I'm not very good, I can't do it. Someone else is so much better than I am, just let them do it."

Sound familiar? Many of us struggle with confidence and find similar conversations going on in our minds. This lack of confidence can have a significant impact on our ability to sing at our best.

If you give me two singers, each with equal talent, quality of tone, range, and experience, except that one of them spends the entire song telling himself he's no good, and the other one is taking on the stage like he owns it, fully confident in his delivery, I guarantee that those are going to be two *very* different performances. And I'm not just talking about what we see, but about the sound that comes out of each of those singers as a result of their different mental, spiritual, and emotional approaches.

Here's what Diana says about her experience after developing her confidence through training: "I'm doing a lot more self talk, telling myself, 'I can do this, I can get better at this, I can succeed.' Right before I sing I tell myself, 'Don't hold back, I can reach the notes, I can sing the song.' If I think that I can't do it, then I don't. But if I get that out of the way and tell myself, 'I can do this, I can sing this,' I get freed—my voice just frees up and I'm able to do it."

Distorted Truth

Many singers do not have an accurate perspective on their vocal ability and how an audience or congregation receives them. If *American Idol* has taught us anything, it's shown us people's capacity for self-deception, right?!

A few times over the years, singers have walked into my studio and I've had to reach up, grab their heels, and plant their feet squarely back in reality. But they are rare exceptions to the norm.

Most of the singers I have worked with who have a distorted perspective on their potential are their own worst critics. They hear one thing while the rest of us experience something completely different. This can happen on any level, from brand-new beginners to Grammy Award–winning artists.

In a CBS interview, four-time Grammy Award winner Seal said, "I never think that anything I do is great. I'm the person who makes the record, finishes the record, and I can't listen to it at all." Clearly there is a gap here between what millions of fans hear when they listen to Seal, and the perspective the singer has on his performance. And how many Grammy Awards do you need on the shelf to be able to embrace your talent and enjoy listening to what you are able to do with your voice? The truth is that no amount of external praise can give us a proper perspective; this realization must happen internally.

Somehow Seal has figured out a way to be able to perform at a very high level while he perceives himself to be performing at a much lower level. From a professional perspective, I would say that his self-doubt isn't detrimental to his performance. But for most of the singers I work with, their misperception literally, physically, and noticeably holds them back from achieving what they're already capable of doing. It is not until they can embrace the truth about their talent and ability that they can fully exercise that talent and progress to their full potential.

Emotional Disconnect

I have worked with many singers who approach their singing very safely, with an emotional distance that protects against the possibility of anything getting too messy or vulnerable. They tend to sing with a constant smile on their face (regardless of what the song is actually about), and everything about them and their communication is a little overly "perky," if you know what I mean.

I see this issue come up most frequently in the worship setting. Many singers begin and end every worship set with the same facial expression, using the same hand gestures they did last week, and managing to navigate through the 20-minute set without having felt anything.

I can usually spot them when they walk into my studio. They're neat. They like everything put together and seem to need everything in their lives to be happy. In order for their singing to progress, they need to start rattling those cages and messing things up. Often, I will assign them a song outside of the worship environment, even outside of Christian music altogether. Their worship songs have become safe for them, and allow them to sing without a connection to anything that is truly going on in their lives.

I remember assigning one of these "happy, perky" types an Alanis Morisette song in which the singer was working through some very real, but very messy, emotional content. Of course, the first week the client brought in the song, it was safe and—you guessed it—happy and perky! We had a conversation about the song, about the client, and about her life, and identified some personal experiences that related quite profoundly to what Alanis was expressing in her song. Once the client made the connection and allowed that part of her to show up, the song took on an entirely new character. Now it was real, it was raw, it was true and authentic—and she sounded great! She did things with her voice that she had never done before. It was amazing! Then all we had to do was to figure out how to bring Alanis with her to church.

It's risky to bring all of who we are to the songs we sing. It gets messy sometimes. It stirs things up while we're standing on stage in front of strangers that it's uncomfortable to feel. But that is where the power of song has the potential to move people, to stir hearts and even to change lives.

Have you been moved by a performance that you observed? I doubt that you would be reading a book on developing your singing voice if you hadn't. Think of the most powerful performance of a song you have ever experienced. And think of the singer who sang that song. Was it a safe performance? Was the singer just recreating notes and words, or was he or she invested and taking risks and putting his or her entire heart and soul out there on the stage?

If we show up, God shows up—every time! And if He shows up, that's when music has power—heart-opening, life-changing, transformational power!

Comparison

I was 18 years old and was in the middle of orientation week at the conservatory of music where I studied for my undergraduate degree. The dean of the conservatory had scheduled a time to meet with the entire group of incoming freshman music majors to share a few words with us before our education began that next week. I don't remember much of what he shared, but I will never forget one story he told us that day.

He had been sitting in his office that spring when his administrator buzzed through his intercom to inform him that his 11:00 A.M. appointment had arrived. In walked an oboe performance major with a stack of papers in her hand. She sat at his desk across from him and announced that she had decided to pursue a psychology degree the next year and needed his signature in order to be able to transfer out of the conservatory and register for classes for that fall.

Something in him felt like there was more to this story. So he asked a few questions and they talked, and eventually, out it all came. There was another oboe performance major at the conservatory. She had perfect tone and incredible musicianship, and no matter how hard this girl worked she felt that she would never be as good as her colleague. If she couldn't be the best oboe player in the conservatory, how would she ever compete for a job in a symphony after she graduated?

They talked for a while longer and the dean asked her to think about her decision for a couple of weeks. There was plenty of time for him to sign her papers, but he asked her to do a little soul searching before they pulled the trigger.

The next week the dean was notified of the arrival of his 3:00 P.M. appointment, and in walked the other oboe performance major, with a stack of papers in her hand! She sat down and told the dean of her intention to transfer out of the conservatory and pursue a business degree because of this other oboe performance major who had perfect tone, incredible musicianship, and on and on.

So here they were, looking over the fence at one another and seeing a different talent, with different strengths. The problem lay in their conclusion that the other person's talent meant that what they had was no good—a conclusion that made them want to give up and quit. What a tragedy that would have been!

Comparison can be a very valuable tool for us in the pursuit of developing our full potential. We should always be on the lookout for talent that will inspire and challenge us to take steps and grow as artists. But we must always practice the discipline of delighting in the gifts and talents and uniqueness that we bring to the world, and savor the opportunity to be the best *us* that we can be!

Fear

Another client of mine says, "The primary thing I needed to overcome in my singing was fear. I think the first time I sang in class, I couldn't breathe. My heart was pounding so hard that it was actually interfering with my lungs working or something. Through the process of just showing up and doing it over and over and over, and getting encouraging comments and constructive feedback, that has really helped me move beyond that."

She faced her fear head-on and made some amazing progress. But the benefit for her didn't end with her singing.

She says, "I feel a whole lot less fear—about everything! I feel like now I can do physical things that were scary for me. I don't know if I'd go as far as bungee jumping, but I feel like I overcame my fear of singing, and I'm doing it! That has made a lot of difference for me in my confidence to choose to do other things in my life that are a little bit scary."

As I said earlier, diving headlong into the process of developing your voice is never just about singing. And when singers face the issues that come up in the process, not only will this make them better singers, it makes them better people. I think it should be a requirement for everyone in the world to study singing. It would be really good job security for me, but beyond that, there is something about singing that provides an environment where the issues that are just below the surface can come up to the top and stare us right in the face. It gives us an opportunity to face what some of us have been running from our entire lives.

I think this is partly because of the personal nature of singing. We don't play an instrument that you can put in a box at the end of the day and lock in the closet. You are the instrument, it's a part of you, and everything about you is going to affect and be affected by your singing. If there are issues in you, they will surface, and you will have the wonderful opportunity to address them and not only unleash your vocal ability, but also become more and more of the person you were designed to be.

Perfectionism

Perfectionism is the pursuit of excellence gone bad. When we take not making a mistake as our primary objective, we make it impossible for our full potential ever to come through in our singing. It is only when we are fearless, taking risks and putting it all out there, that our voices can achieve their highest potential. Mistakes are a part of the ball game, and actually a welcome one.

Did you know that, with all of the pitch correction technology that has come out in recent years, producers will intentionally keep a recording just a little "off"? If they pitch-correct to the point of perfection, the voice no longer sounds human. It loses its life and authenticity.

Even speaking strictly from a technique standpoint, there are things that a singer simply cannot do without jumping off the edge of the cliff and making mistakes, over and over and over again. It's by going too far and making mistakes that we find where the edge is, discover our limitations, and solidify the approach that allows us to sing our best. If we end up singing too much from our head, calculating the approach to perfection, just like an athlete trying to "think" his or her way through the swing of the bat, we will never unleash the energy and abandon required to pull off what we are truly capable of achieving.

Critical Voices

Many singers have allowed someone else to set a limit on what they can or cannot accomplish with their voice. Some singers have let a single experience define their vocal career and their view of themselves and their potential. We play memories like movies in our minds, voices from the past reminding us *not* to believe in ourselves.

I have a client in the Chicago area who says, "In high school I auditioned for a jazz swing choir and got crushed in that audition. I experienced a lot of humiliation, and there is still a voice in my head that says, 'You can't do this! Remember that experience that you had? You struggled with this in high school, you're going to struggle with it now.' It's just always there. I draw back. I get tense. All the things that I know about technique don't matter. It all goes out the window."

Many of us can relate to these kinds of situations that stay with us and limit our ability to do what we know on a deeper level we are capable of.

One of my favorite stories of someone who overcame an external limitation came from my graduate school voice instructor, Dr. Ronald Combs. Ron received what could have been a defining evaluation from an important adult figure in his life, but before I share that, let me tell you a little about Dr. Combs. Ron is, in my opinion, the greatest vocal pedagogue living today. He is better read on the subject than anyone I have ever met and is a master at making this vast knowledge applicable and understandable to his students. Ron received his doctorate in voice from Northwestern University in Evanston, Illinois, one of the finest music schools in the country. As a singer he has performed with professional opera companies throughout the Midwest. As a teacher he has taught professional opera singers as well as Tony and Grammy Award winners. I know of clients who fly from as far away as Germany to study with the man. In a word, he is simply brilliant.

When Ron was in elementary school, his choir director pulled him aside and told him that he thought Ron was most likely tone-deaf, and that there really wasn't much of a future for him in this whole singing thing. He suggested that Ron would be better off pursuing another elective as an alternative. Much like Michael Jordan being cut when he tried out for his high school basketball team, I'm sure that this only fueled the determination that has made Dr. Combs such a success.

But many of us allow these experiences and voices to limit our potential. We need to rise above these parameters, record new voices to be played in our head, and trust the talent and ability that we know we possess.

Lack of Trust

Every once in a while I experience the gift of having someone I'm working with take the risk of letting me know about the internal dynamics he or she is working through as these relate to singing. Some of these singers have shared with me stories from their life that have made it difficult for them to approach anyone or anything in their life with open hands and trust. They've leaned their weight into people, or dreams, or other pursuits before and they know what it feels like to taste pavement as trust was broken and things came crashing down. I've also seen these people do tremendous work and finally put an end to running from this issue in their life; they stop, plant their feet, square up, and face it head-on. They've found the ability to risk again, trust, and take the leap. And the results have been amazing to witness. As with every issue we have discussed, they become different people through the process and their voices are transformed!

It is impossible to accomplish certain aspects of successful singing without trust. It's a scary thing to put your voice out there, to lean in and not hold back. It's much safer to keep things reeled in and only express what is safe and comfortable with your voice. But once a singer takes the leap and trusts with the whole heart and the entire body, vocal range increases, dynamics expand, intonation improves, the tone finds a sparkle, and the voice is able to soar. But none of that can happen with your feet still firmly planted on the edge of the cliff. It requires trust. It requires a jump.

Stage Fright

Stage fright is a big one. Every singer I've ever worked with deals with it. And it limits our potential! So many singers know what they sound like at home, with the windows closed, the shades drawn, and the doors locked. And yet they just can't seem to perform at that level when the pressure is on. We've all experienced the effects of it right before we walk onto the stage: sweaty palms, shortness of breath, nausea, dry mouth, panic, heart palpitations, and on and on. It's a wonder that any of us stick with it, with all of these marvelous things that come along with singing!

One of the most important things I've discovered while researching this and reading interviews and memoirs by some of the best of the best that have ever walked the planet (folks like Luciano Pavarotti and Barbra Streisand) is that the goal is *not* to not get nervous. I know, it's a double negative, but did you catch it? The goal is *not* to not get nervous. So many singers can be heard backstage, telling themselves, "Okay, just settle down, relax. You're going to be okay. Just breathe, you can do this!" They spend an enormous amount of energy trying to talk themselves out of being nervous.

But the best of the best describe the ability to take all of that nervous energy and focus it in a way that allows them to perform at higher levels then they can ever replicate in rehearsal. Their range increases, they can hold notes longer, they sing with more power and more control. All of the energy that is bubbling at the surface and requiring many of them to firmly grasp the porcelain with both hands moments before walking on the stage is the very energy that allows them to function at their best. So an important first step in dealing with nervous energy is to change our relationship to it and welcome it in as a resource that will help us. If we can focus that energy in a way that is constructive and not self-defeating, nervous energy can become one of our greatest allies.

Some other things that help us manage stage fright are:

1. **Laugh**
   It is amazing how much we can benefit from maintaining our sense of humor. I used to perform with a friend at Willow Creek, who was not only one of the most talented musicians I have ever worked with, but also one of the funniest people I've met. He was always pulling stunts, like one time when he untucked my shirt just before we stepped out in front of the side curtain and onto the stage in front of 5,000 people. As I tried frantically to get myself put back together while walking onto the stage to grab my mic, I couldn't help but laugh and be reminded to lighten up and not take myself so seriously. Another time I was singing a solo to close a service. Bill Hybels, our pastor, was closing his sermon in prayer and I was going to sing the song that was intended to allow everything he'd been talking about to sink into the hearts of everyone that was there. As Bill was praying, I looked up and there was my buddy at the piano, making a face at me, just doing whatever he could to make me laugh. And it worked. Every time he'd pull one of his stunts, I'd laugh, my heart would lighten, and I'd be freed up to just relax and do what I was already capable of doing.

2. **Just Breathe**
   The low diaphragmatic breathing technique I explained earlier not only allows us to provide maximum energy to our voice, it is also a great tool for relaxation. Psychologists use that same breathing technique when they work with patients dealing with depression and anxiety because of the natural calming effect it has over the entire body.

3. **Focus**
   Whenever stage fright has a paralyzing effect on our potential as singers, we have allowed ourselves to become more focused on ourselves than on what we are singing about and who we are singing to. When we are vitally connected to the meaning of the songs we sing, and we feel that internal connection and passion to express our hearts through our song, we lose our preoccupation with ourselves and rise above fear and nervous energy to get lost in the connection between ourselves, the music, and our audience.

4. Prepare

Often there is good reason for us to be nervous and afraid of walking on the stage. We simply haven't prepared to the degree we need to, and there is nothing more terrifying than walking onto a stage knowing that you're going to have to get lucky in order to pull this one off. One of the goals I have for myself in preparing for a big performance is to be able to have a conversation with myself right before I walk onto the stage. I want to be able to look myself in the eye in the bathroom mirror and say, "You have done everything you could have possibly done to prepare for this moment. What happens now is beyond your control. You've worked hard for this, now go out there and enjoy it!" There have been plenty of times when I've had to dodge myself in that mirror because I haven't done my homework, but the times I've been able to have that conversation, I feel a confidence that frees me up to get out there and do my best.

Lea Salonga, who has played many roles on Broadway and in Disney movies, gave an interview to *Broadway Beat* on March 17, 2007, about playing the role of Fantine in *Les Misérables* on Broadway. In particular, she was discussing the song "I Dreamed a Dream," the experience of singing it, and how she prepared for it. She says, "'I Dreamed a Dream,' it's a jewel to wrap one's voice around. But when you first look at the lyrics without reading the book, just as a song, you see it as a love song. She's talking about regret, she's talking about a man she loved—but when you read the actual Victor Hugo novel there's so much more information. The singing and interpreting of it becomes different and more meaty and there's just more weight after reading the novel. Not even watching the show for me would do it; it was reading the book."

My edition of Victor Hugo's novel *Les Misérables* has 1,167 pages! Reading a novel was part of the process that allowed her to really connect to a character and effectively communicate the essence of a song. Preparation! In comparison to the example set by Lea Salonga, many of us should be terrified when we walk onto the stage, because we have not put in nearly the time and preparation we need to perform the material at our best.

Many singers in modern worship are lazy. They spend minimal time in rehearsal, usually figuring that if they've memorized the words and don't mess up the notes, they're good. When we prepare to the point where the song is a part of us, and we have interacted with it, allowed the song to speak to us and penetrate our heart (which happens way after we've memorized notes and words), it is amazing how little control stage fright has over our performance. We are able to step onto the stage with confidence, allowing nervous energy to elevate our ability as we boldly communicate the message that has been burned into our heart through song.

Overcoming Internal Issues

Identifying the issues listed above that you feel have an effect on your voice and development is an important first step. We want to identify the problems that plague us so that we can move through them, get on to bigger and better things, and realize the full potential in our voice and in who we can become as individuals. But awareness is only the beginning. Many singers never move beyond these personal barriers to experience the freedom and liberation awaiting them on the other side.

We will take a look at three keys that singers I know have used to help them move beyond the limitations that hold them back. What follows are merely my observations and in no way a suggestion that these keys will unlock all of the issues mentioned above. I am a vocal coach and not a professional counselor or a spiritual director. I understand the depth and complexity that some of these personal challenges can hold. I will recommend now and later in our discussion that people seek out professional help when they need assistance in navigating the path to freedom. That said, here are three observations of what I believe can be extremely helpful tools in overcoming the barriers we face.

The Importance of Community

The singers I have worked with who have looked to others for help, support, and sometimes just a friend to talk things through with, have moved through the issues that hold them back exponentially faster than those who try to go it alone. Having trusted people in your life whom you can tell about the challenges that you come up against can be an invaluable resource in helping you talk through the inner dynamics of what is really happening for you. They can offer advice and a perspective from the outside that we simply can't provide for ourselves, and they can offer encouragement to help us keep going, even when things get hard.

Sometimes a singer bumps up against barriers that require more than a few trusted friends to help them navigate the challenges. It can be a really good idea to seek out professional help from a trained psychologist or counselor who has spent years learning about the issue you face and helping others to overcome the bondage and limitations that come with it.

Whatever resources you need, seek them out, whether it's a professional, a group of friends, or a mentor. We were clearly not created to live in isolation. We need community around us, and it will be an important key to our success.

Sing!

The more you sing, the more the issue is going to come up. The more the issue comes up, the more you have an opportunity to set it down and move beyond it. To a certain degree it's all about reps—the more you do it, the faster you get to the good stuff.

Create opportunities for yourself to sing! Sing for your friends. Lead a time of worship for your small group. I have seen entire ministries begin out of a selfish need for someone to just have a "gig" and an opportunity to work on his or her voice.

At Willow Creek there is always something going on every night of the week. And at a place the size of Willow Creek, we had sub-ministries that would meet on a weeknight in as large a gathering as you would find at many churches. One of those ministries was a 12-week program designed to assist people who were grieving a death in their life. It was an amazing ministry and the impact it had was tremendous. One of my clients at the time was looking for an opportunity to do some more singing. She wasn't singing at the level required for the main services, but she had a talent that could be a blessing to many others, and she needed to use it. I knew that this ministry was also in need of someone who could sing an occasional song as a part of their program. I connected the two and it was magic. My client was thrilled at the opportunity and loved what she got to do. It gave her a regular outlet that she had as a motivation to work on songs and develop her voice, and the ministry leader was thrilled with how much it added to their program. In the years to come my client caught a larger vision and recruited a full band, then a lighting and sound team, and even some folks to help with video and drama. They developed a full curriculum for this program, complete with music, playscripts, and videos. These resources ended up not only serving this program at Willow Creek, but eventually being distributed to churches all over the world—all as a result of what had begun as a simple need to get more reps singing a gig.

Be creative, and look for opportunities to sing worship in places other than your main church services. There are opportunities all around you—opportunities that will not only benefit you and your vocal and personal development, but will also allow you to bless others with your gift and passion for singing!

Courageously Face Barriers

I have seen singers take the first step in the process, and identify the barriers that are holding back their potential. Usually they didn't have much of a choice because those issues jumped up right in front of their face. Then I've seen these singers tread water, sometimes for years, making little to no progress. Why? The reasons can vary slightly, but the main theme is that they are avoiding the problem. They are standing on the edge of the deep end and just dipping a toe in the water. I understand, because facing the challenges in our lives is never fun. It's scary, uncomfortable, sometimes expensive, and unsettling. It's like a journey through the valley of the shadow of death. But setting up camp in the valley of the shadow of death isn't fun, either!

I have also watched as singers dove into the deep end to face their fears with an aggressive determination, intent on not allowing these barriers to hold back their potential any longer. What happens for these singers is that they move through the valley of the shadow of death much faster, and before they know it they are in the Promised Land on the other side!

Whatever your issue is, I encourage you to dive in and face it. Terrifying as it may be, it is the only path to realizing your full potential as a singer and as a human being. Don't settle for anything less than what you are capable of, and boldly go after anything that is holding you back. I have had a front row seat to this amazing process hundreds of times, and not one of those singers regrets the grass they get to play in on the other side of the valley, in the Promised Land!

10

The Characteristics of a Worship Vocalist

Be a Person of Integrity

"Let your 'Yes' be yes, and your 'No,' no" (James 5:12, NIV).

There are a lot of games played in the music world. People will do or say whatever they need to in order to get to the top. Don't let that be what characterizes you or your involvement as a worship vocalist. Be who you are and say what is so. Live a life of congruency between what is inside of you and what is outside of you. Let your actions, everything you say and do, flow out of a genuine heart. And if what shows up on the outside isn't what you want others to see, clean up the inside! Do the internal work that you need to do to open yourself to the Light of God that can transform you into the person you were truly created to be.

Follow through on your commitments. If you say you're going to sing for a service, show up and do it. If you say that you're going to be at a rehearsal at 7:00 P.M., be there at 6:45 P.M. In the professional music world, there is a zero tolerance policy on canceling a gig or showing up late to a rehearsal or session. There's a good chance that if it happens, it's the last time you'll get the call. The worship environment shouldn't be any different, and don't you think that the standard should be even higher?

Tell the truth. Follow through on your word. Cultivate a heart full of God's love and goodness, and allow that to pour through all of who you are!

Encourage Your Teammates and Leadership

"The body is a unit, though it is made up of many parts; and though all its parts are many, they form one body. God has put the body together. If one part suffers, every part suffers with it; if one part is honored, every part rejoices with it" (1 Corinthians 12:12, 24, 26, NIV).

A worship team should be an environment where each one of us experiences some of the greatest encouragement and support that we will ever receive as singers. We should all be each other's biggest fans!

We all win when we check our egos at the door and show up free to simply bring our best and celebrate the talents and abilities that we see in the other members of the team around us.

Take the time to go out of your way to let someone know how much you enjoy hearing her voice on the alto part and what a great addition it is to the team. Pull someone aside and tell him how the joy and enthusiasm he shows up with every week is contagious and that you're really glad you get to serve alongside him. Drop your worship leader a note in the mail, thanking him or her for using his or her gifts in ministry and working so hard to lead your team and provide a place for others to serve.

These small gestures not only benefit our team members, they cultivate in our own hearts an openness and embracing quality that keeps us away from the trap of competition and comparison, freeing us up to savor and enjoy our unique gifts the way we are encouraging others to do the same.

Always Be Refining Your Skill

"'Well done, good and faithful servant. You have been faithful over a little; I will set you over much. Enter into the joy of your master'" (Matthew 25:23, ESV).

There is no arrival point on the path of vocal development. An athlete doesn't get to stop preparing for marathons after training for 20 years. Being the best singer you can be is a lifelong pursuit. It's exciting that you can always be growing and learning and expanding as a singer over your entire life! We should all be constantly working to refine our gifts, taking on the next level in our ability, and striving to bring nothing less than our absolute best to singing worship.

The church used to be the pinnacle of the arts community. The best art in the world came out of the church. The church set the standard. There was a "worship leader" at a church in Leipzig, Germany, named Johann Sebastian Bach. He did some decent stuff. There's a little painting on a ceiling of a church in Rome, Italy, called the Sistine Chapel, that was painted by a guy named Michelangelo. It's pretty good, too. Sadly, today the church features some of the most uninspiring art you can find anywhere. You can head down to a local pub on a Friday night and hear better music than you will hear at the church around the corner on Sunday morning. A big part of this is due to the fact that the artists in the church are not passionately pursuing the development and expression of their gifts.

Don't be complacent, and offer on Sunday morning something that has cost you nothing. As a singer in the church, strive to constantly be the best that you can be, and display the full potential of the gifts that God has given to you.

Have a Spiritual Mentor

"Iron sharpens iron, and one man sharpens another" (Proverbs 27:17, ESV).

We all need guidance and direction in our lives. Seek out someone you can share anything and everything with. Someone who can listen but also challenge you and encourage you to live the life you are called to. Find someone whom you connect with, trust, and respect. These people are out there, and they can be invaluable once you have them in your life. But because of their wisdom and discernment, they aren't going to be advertising themselves, or pushing this opportunity on you. You are going to have to do the searching and initiate the request. Be very specific about the kind of person you are looking for, the role that you feel you need him or her to play in your life, and begin asking God to direct you to this person. The person will appear, as long as you are looking and asking, at exactly the moment he or she is needed.

Live Healthy

"Your bodies are temples of the Holy Spirit" (1 Corinthians 6:19, NIV).

One of the amazing things about singing is that it involves all of who we are. Every aspect of our life shows up in the way we sing. Because of this, it is critical that we take care of ourselves—all of ourselves. We need to eat well, exercise regularly, get adequate sleep, and care for our emotional and spiritual lives. Take the time to do an inventory on each of these areas in your life. How are you doing? What can you do to make some improvements in the areas you feel are lacking? You may need to change up your diet, or start working out three times a week. You'll be amazed at how much better you feel, and what a positive effect it will have on your singing voice.

Sing Outside of the Church

"So wherever you go in the world, tell everyone the Good News" (Mark 16:15, GWT).

Many singers are frustrated because their involvement in church doesn't fulfill their desire to use their voices. And once they begin the development process it surely isn't providing enough opportunities to work out the issues that they are facing. I believe that it is important for every worship singer (even full-time staff members) to be regularly singing outside of the church. This gives us an opportunity to bring our light outside the walls of our church. It keeps us well rounded as singers, and broadens our vocal experience and versatility. You'll experience a different kind of pressure, different expectations, and a different audience to sing to and work with. These opportunities will make you better, keep you sharp, and give you fresh ideas and energy to bring back with you to the worship environment.

The Church Doesn't Exist for You to Have a Gig!

It also helps to keep a really important fact in mind: the church doesn't exist so that you can have a place to perform! A lot of things in ministry get messy when singers start looking to the church as their sole outlet to sing and fulfill all of their needs and desires as vocal artists. Competition begins to arise, because in order to have your musical and vocal needs met, you need to beat out anyone else who might compete for the opportunities you need to stay fulfilled. And when those opportunities go to someone else, resentment easily builds toward others on your team. Not only does this strain relationships and morale in our worship communities, but we also miss out on the chance to freely and enthusiastically celebrate the success and talent of others on our team. We should be each other's biggest cheerleaders and support, and it's hard to do that that when there is a twinge of resentment in our heart.

It is amazing what happens when a singer who is frustrated with the church because of a lack of opportunities gets out there and finds success in some different venues. You'll find this will give you more freedom to enjoy serving at church, because it's not the only spout you are looking to in order to fill your cup. Suddenly you are freed up to approach your role in the church with open arms and a pure heart, ready to contribute in whatever way the leadership of the team feels is best. You are getting positive encouragement and validation of your gifts and abilities from a broader source and not looking to the worship leader or vocal director as the authority who defines your ability and talent.

The Heart of the Artist

For further reading on the subject of character and team dynamics in ministry, I highly recommend Rory Noland's book *The Heart of the Artist* as a must-read for every worship vocalist.

11

For the Vocal Director or Worship Leader

Leading the singers in your worship ministry is a challenging endeavor. Many worship leaders feel like they are not really sure what to do with this subculture within the team. Singers are different from the other members of the band and tech team. They have different emotional needs. They think and speak about music differently. They hang out and relate differently. Sound about right? Don't worry, there are some simple principles that will help you understand these unique creatures and allow you to effectively lead them and create an environment where their gifts and talents can flourish. We'll take a look at four major aspects of what is required to successfully lead singers in our worship ministry: auditions, rehearsals, community, and development.

Audition Process

An audition process is an important aspect of any successful worship ministry. It is critical that we set a standard for who we are inviting onto our team. It's never a good scenario when we realize we have allowed people on our team who aren't really equipped to serve at the level that we need them to. We need to have a process that sets the standard for the skill level we are expecting on our team.

Auditions do a lot more than give you an excuse to go "Simon Cowell" on someone. They give you a chance to define your own standards and expectations for the team you are building. They provide an opportunity for you to get to know singers before you drop them into the middle of your ministry and onto the stage of your church, and they give you the chance to communicate clearly and directly to new team members about what they are going to be a part of and what their role will be prior to them getting started.

Tremendous good can come from a well-structured audition process, both for the ministry and for the new members being added to the team. You will be communicating a lot to potential team members about who you are as a ministry throughout the process, and you want to do all you can to make sure that you are sending the right message.

I can remember times at Willow Creek when our audition process lacked vision and organization. As a staff we were so focused on just surviving Sunday services, conferences, and special events that we didn't have a regular schedule of when auditions would take place, or a clear process outlined for what the auditions would look like—including who was responsible for making them happen. Congregation members who wanted to audition as singers might be transferred around from one staff person to another for weeks before getting any clear answers on how to begin. And I remember one singer—eventually one of the best we had at Willow—whose application sat in a file cabinet for over a year before we got back to her.

But when things were functioning at their best, the process was clearly defined, and everyone answering the phones knew exactly where to send people for more information. The auditions themselves were a beautiful process where people were honored, challenged, respected, and addressed with honesty and love. Almost all the singers we heard walked out of the audition even more in love with the church they were called to, and even clearer and more excited than ever to refine their gifts and improve their vocal ability—even if we told them that they hadn't made the team!

If you don't have an audition process, you need one! I hope this section provides you with some practical tools for establishing a process that will work in your unique ministry setting. If you already have an audition process, I hope this will provide some ideas to help you refine your process and encourage you to stay true to the values that define and support your ministry.

Defining Team Values

The first step in establishing an audition process is to clarify who you are as a team, and then define your expectations for the type of person you want to bring onto the team. As an artist, I have a natural aversion to things like corporate structure and Excel spreadsheets. However, sometimes definition and structure can be a very good thing. It can be a real benefit to you and your ministry to take the time to write a mission statement that spells out in black and white the values of your ministry, and what characteristics and expectations define you and the members of your team.

In establishing a mission statement for your ministry it is important to look at the values of the church you serve within. Does your church have a mission statement? This would be a good place to start to ensure that everything you establish as a team is in alignment with the overarching values of the church.

Here are some questions that will help you determine your mission statement as a team:

1. What purpose do you serve as a team?
2. How will you fulfill that purpose?
3. What are the characteristics that define you as a team?

It is important to think of these things in a few different categories:

Vocal and Music Ability

Is it important that your singers be able to read music? Pick up harmonies by ear? Sing a variety of styles? Sing one particular style really well? Be able to sing in chest voice? Have a certain range? Be comfortable and charismatic on stage?

Think through questions like these and others that fit the needs of your ministry.

Emotional and Relational Maturity

Come up with a sentence or two to describe the type of person you want on your team. What are you looking for in terms of relational and emotional maturity? Then make sure your process allows you an opportunity to access this. It's important to get to know the people you are auditioning. Talk with them. See them around other members of your team.

Check their references (ideally, speak to their small group leader) and get a feel for the relational patterns your candidates use in other settings.

Spiritual Maturity

What are your expectations in terms of the spiritual maturity of the members on your team? Is it okay for them to still be exploring Christianity, or do you want the singers in your ministry to be fully devoted followers of Christ? Should they be in a small group? What lifestyle characteristics do you expect to see in the members of your team?

These are important things to clarify and spell out. It will help you to see your values written out on a sheet of paper as you consider whether your ministry truly reflects those values, or if you need to make some adjustments. These definitions will also help you to clearly communicate your expectations to new (and existing) team members.

Application

The first thing someone should receive when inquiring about being a part of your team is a letter from you as the leader of your worship ministry (or in some cases the vocal director in charge of the audition process) and an application to be filled out and returned at the audition.

Your letter should be both welcoming and informative. You want people to know that you are excited to get to know them and their gifts. You also want to provide people with a clear idea of what to expect in the process, how to sign up for an audition, and how soon they will be notified of your decision after the auditions take place. You also want to think through what exactly you'll have them sing at the audition. Some worship leaders have them choose from a few different songs that you use in your service and to be ready to sing melody as well as harmonize on the song(s). This can be a good approach. I like to have singers prepare two songs (one up-tempo selection and one ballad) on their own in a style that is consistent with the songs you use in your services. Performance songs often show a little more range and style than the typical worship chorus, and this will allow singers the opportunity to introduce you to their personality and vocal strengths. Have them bring in a background accompaniment (karaoke track) for the audition.

Your application should capture singers' contact information and provide them with an opportunity to tell you about their singing background, spiritual journey, and motivations for joining the ministry.

Day of Auditions

Facilitating auditions can be tricky. You have an objective in mind; you are evaluating every person who walks through the audition room door to determine whether he or she can sing with the technique, style, and musicianship you require and can demonstrate the character qualities you are expecting from everyone on your team. But it's not an *American Idol* audition, it's the church, and you want to honor and respect people and communicate the truth in love. So what are some key components of your audition day that will help you do that? There are a lot of ways to do this, but here is the format I use when conducting auditions:

Make It a Team Effort

I do not ever do auditions alone—ever! Have at least one (and I always prefer to have two) other people in the room with you for auditions. Make sure that you have both a man and a woman represented, and choose people on your team to help. Choose based on intuition and emotional and spiritual maturity, rather than vocal ability—and choose people you trust and can relax and have fun with. You never know what situation is going to come walking through the door. You want people in the room with you who will have your back, handle everything with grace and class, and be able to lighten the tension with an appropriate amount of levity.

A Check-in Location

In addition to the person or people in the room with you, also choose someone from your team to serve as the monitor, and another person to relay people back and forth to the audition room. You want to have an area designated for people to check in, confirm their time, and receive instructions on where they can wait until they're called in. You want your monitor to be someone who will greet everyone with a smile, help the nervous auditioners relax, and yet have enough backbone and structure that they can manage any logistics that come up. Your relay person should also be great with people, and able to lend support, encouragement, and possibly a shoulder to cry on with every person they meet that day.

I think it's a great idea to have a "holding" area where people can wait for their audition time, and then to have them escorted to and from their audition in a separate location. It's great if you can have an exit for people after the audition that doesn't require them to pass by everyone waiting in the holding area. Auditions can sometimes be very stressful, and a lot of emotion can come in the wake of an audition. It will be best if your relay person can not only bring singers to the audition location, but also be there afterward to escort them to the exit before returning to get the next person.

Audition Process

As you audition candidates, welcome them, let them know you're glad they are there, and, before they sing, say a prayer for them, asking God to bless them with peace and the ability to show the best representation of the gifts they've been given. Then have them sing what they've prepared. I always think it's a good idea to work with people in the audition, especially if you think they have potential. If you want them to try a section again, give them some clear instructions and adjustments to make, and have them give that section another shot. This may reveal a voice that's been hiding behind a load of nervous energy, and it gives you a chance to see how candidates respond to coaching, both personally and vocally. Once you are done, ask them to leave the room for a moment and have your relay person ready to greet them and connect with them while they wait. Once they leave, this is a chance for you and your fellow auditors to discuss what you've just heard and make a decision on the next step. For me, this means either letting singers know they didn't make the team, or inviting them to a callback.

Once you bring a singer back into the room I would share your decision in person, right there that day. For singers who don't make the team, give specific reasons why. If they've only been coming to the church for three months and haven't joined a small group or gotten involved at all, but they have a great voice, let them know that you'd like to see them get more involved in the community and re-audition in three to six months. If there are specific things about a person's voice that aren't at the level that you need them to be, explain specifically what those things are. Giving people the gift of truth covered in love is a beautiful thing. They may be completely tone-deaf and lacking the ability to match a single pitch. If that's what you heard, then you should tell them that. If they have a nice voice, but lack strength, or sing with the wrong style for your services, tell them exactly that! It seems risky to do this, but I have found that it clears up a lot of confusion and uncertainty for people, and I honestly can't think of a single time this approach has backfired. Have resources and recommendations available to give to those who are interested in developing their gifts. You may be amazed when you see people come back after six months of hard work and blow you away with their progress. That's why I'm in the business that I'm in—it's not only possible, it happens every day!

If you think you're going to bring someone onto the team, do not give him or her the invitation that day, even if Chris Tomlin walks through the door. I think it communicates a lot about how seriously you take bringing someone onto the team when you have singers come to a second audition. When you invite candidates to a callback, give them some things to work on for that callback. Everyone has room for improvement, and even if it's just to demonstrate a different style than what they brought into their first audition, give them an assignment and something that you'd like them to do differently for next time. If you're not sure they have the chops to be on your team because of some vocal things that came up, give clear feedback on exactly what you are wanting to hear differently—and give candidates the opportunity to ask for clarification on what they need to do to show you they have what it takes. Occasionally, you'll come across an amazing voice and for whatever reason someone in the room has some red flags that come up about the singer personally. Always pay attention to those things, and don't be afraid to push the pause button on the process when they come up. I can remember some world-class singers who came through auditions at Willow Creek, and we would get the sense that their motivation had more to do with the chance to sing in front of 20,000 people on the weekend than it did with a heart that truly wanted to serve. Or we thought we spotted some prima donna tendencies and wondered how this person would work with others on the team. I've asked people to come and be a part of a small group for a couple of months with other singers on the worship team before they were invited to join. They met weekly, and the insight I got from that small group leader helped me figure out whether those people (and their phenomenal talent) were really ready to be brought on board.

It's a big deal; take your time on the front end. It's much easier to slow the process down and really get to know someone than it is to deal with the ramifications of having someone on the team, or even removing someone from the team, whom you really shouldn't have brought on in the first place. By taking your time, and paying attention in the audition process, you can save yourself and your ministry a lot of heartache and stress.

The process can be two auditions and just a matter of a week or two, or it can take months and involve numerous auditions—you get to decide when you're ready to bring someone on. Just communicate openly and honestly throughout the entire process. It's when people feel that things are being withheld or that you're not shooting straight that issues can come up.

When you bring someone on the team, make a big deal about it. Choose a proper time to welcome the new person and introduce him or her to the entire team at once. Celebrate new members' introduction and make them feel like they've just joined the greatest team in the world, because that's the kind of team you're building.

Rehearsals

The way you approach your rehearsals will have a significant impact on the success of your ministry. A productive rehearsal process will nurture your singers' talents and abilities. It will offer a structure that respects their time, encourages them to show up and work hard, and allows them to enjoy rich community. A great rehearsal should have everyone leaving energized and excited about being a part of the ministry. Here are some ideas that will help you structure your rehearsals in a way that creates that kind of enthusiasm and productivity.

Rehearse Separately

One of the most important things you can do to increase the efficiency and effectiveness of your rehearsals is to rehearse singers separately from the instrumentalists. Leading instrumentalists and leading vocalists are completely different ball games. You'll be addressing different issues with each group, and wasting the time of one group while you're attending to the needs of the other. By working exclusively with your singers you can focus on the aspects of their role that are unique, and cultivate an environment that will prepare them in a way that a joint rehearsal simply cannot.

This doesn't mean that the singers and band never mix prior to service time, but dedicating a time to work separately prior to a joint rehearsal will have a tremendous impact on the freedom your singers feel to lead worship, and the joy and confidence they will experience in serving. Too often, vocalists are just thrown in with the band and expected to figure out their problems, while much of the attention in the rehearsal is dedicated to the instrumentalists. Rehearsing your singers separately from your instrumentalists before bringing the two groups together makes your rehearsals more productive, efficient, and fun!

Characteristics of an Effective Vocal Rehearsal

Here are the important things that singers need in order to feel prepared and equipped to lead worship with excellence and heart.

Learn Parts

Singers need to know when they are supposed to sing harmonies, who is supposed to sing those harmonies, and what those harmonies are. It is important that whoever is leading the rehearsal walk into the room with all of that figured out ahead of time and lead singers through this quickly and efficiently. You need to know your team and be prepared to provide them with the tools they need to be able to accomplish this. Does everyone in the rehearsal read music? Then having a lead sheet with the harmonies already printed is a good idea, and will be all that you need. Do some of the members of the team for that week learn harmonies only by ear? Then make sure that you cover all of the places where they will be singing harmony and have them bring in some type of recording device that they can use to capture their part during rehearsal. Are you dealing with singers who can just pick stuff out of the air, harmonize on the fly, and feel comfortable and confident doing so? Consider yourself lucky and use your rehearsal time to focus on other aspects of helping them to prepare.

Singers' needs vary significantly in this area. You need to know the needs of each individual on your team and come into rehearsal prepared. Move through this part of the rehearsal quickly, don't let things get bogged down, give them what they need, and send them home to lock it in on their own and come back prepared. It's a delicate balance to give them what they need without allowing this part of the process to monopolize all of your time. The better prepared you are as the rehearsal leader, the more efficiently this portion of the rehearsal will go.

Song Structure

Each worship leader approaches his or her worship leading differently. Leading worship is an outpouring of who you are as an individual, and the way you lead will reflect your own unique personality and character. This is particularly true in the way that the service and the flow of the songs are structured. Some leaders have no idea how the song will actually go until they get up there to lead. Some worship leaders know exactly how many times they will repeat the bridge before they jump back into the chorus—every detail is mapped out.

However you lead is perfect! The important thing in leading singers is that you are preparing them to support your brand of leadership. If you jump all around, be sure to teach them the main sections of each song, and establish clear cues that will allow them to lead with you, not feel like they are holding on tightly to the leash of an enormous dog dragging them around to who knows where. Be sure to dedicate time in rehearsal to jumping around so that those who are unfamiliar with that format can get comfortable co-leading with you, without the pressure of a service and a full congregation in the mix.

If you are more of the structured leader type, then be sure to clearly communicate that structure, and clearly outline the flow of each song, in this part of the rehearsal.

Rehearsing Style

Once you have rehearsed the structure of the song, be sure that your team is equipped to bring the right colors to the painting. Are there sections of the song where you want the dynamics to drop and the singers' tone to get breathy and light? Are there sections where you want the singers to bust out in a full-on gospel sound with chest voice and soulful vibrato? Have you figured out where and when you're going to use stylistic tools like pitch bends and specific diction? Are there individuals who are singing too formally and need some special assistance in order to make the adjustments that will help them lock in with the group?

Isolating specific areas of a song where your singers are challenged stylistically is a great way to lock things into place. Repeat those sections over and over, making adjustments as you coach them in the style you want to hear. Be patient if singers aren't getting it right away, and keep coming at your coaching from different angles. Model for them the stylistic approach you want to hear and have them match that with their vocal approach.

It is important to come into rehearsal with a vision of where you want the song to go and what stylistic adjustments your singers will need to make in order to lead with the sound you are looking for. Take a look before rehearsal at the team you will be leading, and be prepared to offer help to singers whom you know are more deficient in this area.

Opening the Heart

Learning the parts and working on style are just the nuts and bolts of what singers need in a rehearsal. That's the easy stuff, the aspects of their role that sit on the surface. The most important thing you will do in a rehearsal is to create an opportunity where your singers' pulses can drop, all the things spinning around in their minds can settle, and they can descend into and open their hearts. It's important for us to provide an opportunity in our rehearsals for our singers to open and connect their hearts to the message of the songs they will be singing so that they are prepared to do the same thing as they lead the congregation. For some this comes naturally; others need help and guidance. Lead your singers through an exercise that will provide an environment for this to take place:

1. We run our lives at mach speed and come flying into rehearsal (often after a busy and exhausting day). What happens is that we leave parts of ourselves lagging behind. The heart can't move that fast, so it's going require a special environment and invitation for your singers' hearts to finally arrive in the room and climb back into their chests. Provide an opportunity for your singers to completely show up in your rehearsal. Dim the lights and have the singers sit on the floor, close their eyes, breathe deeply, and simply be quiet for a couple of minutes.
2. Once they've connected to their hearts, guide them through a process of bringing their hearts to the lyrics and message of the songs they will be leading. Allow the songs to speak to them and their lives, and invite them to bring all of that to their worship.

This exercise can be played out in hundreds of different ways. Be creative, and take time as you prepare to lead rehearsal to ask the Holy Spirit to guide you in creating an opportunity for these two critical things to happen for your singers. For some of you, guiding your singers in this way may be a brand-new aspect of rehearsals. Here is a sample exercise to get you started:

Have everyone in the rehearsal put down their lead sheets, lyrics, and recording devices. Sit down on the floor in a circle and start with 60 seconds of silence. Have the singers close their eyes and take a moment to ask themselves what area of their life is speaking the loudest in the middle of their silence. What part of each singer's heart is crying out to be heard? Invite them to bring that part of themselves forward. What does it need to say? What does it need to hear?

Invite them to imagine themselves crawling up into the hand of God, and allowing God to fully see and know their hearts.

As they imagine that, still with their eyes closed, slowly, line by line, read the lyrics of the most poignant song they will sing that week, a song that gets at the heart of the worship for that week, and a song that they are familiar with. Read through the entire song without any music or singing, just reading the lyrics. After you have read the song, begin singing it, slowly, and invite them to join in. I am quite sure that the sound you hear and the depth of conviction your singers communicate with will be drastically different from what you heard the first time you sang through that song in rehearsal.

You have invited them to bring their hearts, then guided them through a process of connecting themselves to the true meaning of the song, and you experienced together the power of worshipping with that level of authentic heart engagement. After this part of the exercise you may also want to provide the opportunity for your singers to share some of what stirred in them during the exercise and what things came to the surface. It's very powerful to be on stage leading worship, knowing what is happening in the hearts of the singers around you, and what life circumstances are present in their mind as they are leading worship.

Prepare

If we are going to be successful at leading our rehearsals in all of these areas it is critical that as leaders we come in prepared. Our volunteers are giving their time, and we want to use that time with honor, and efficiently and skillfully lead them through every aspect of what will be required for them to do their best. We can't do that if we come into rehearsal flying by the seat of our pants and just make it up as we go along.

Rehearsal Structure

In order to accomplish every aspect of these rehearsals, having a separate rehearsal for your singers is critical; we can't adequately address each of these areas with a full band in the room. If moving to this format is something new for your ministry structure, it can be challenging to create space for it. There are three main formats in which I have seen different ministries structure their rehearsal process: the *day-of-game process*, the *one-rehearsal process*, and the *two-rehearsal process*. Let's take a look at each process and some ways that we can create space for a singers-only rehearsal.

The Day-of-Game Process

Some ministries are not able to rehearse on a different day than their service time, so they set an early call time and hold the rehearsal immediately prior to the beginning of the service. If there's any way to avoid this format, I would highly recommend adjusting your process to either the one- or two-rehearsal process outlined below. There are a number of downsides to rehearsing the same day as your services.

1. There is a lot of time pressure to cram everything in before the service begins. If a musical issue needs to be addressed or worked through, you can't very easily ask everyone in the church to adjust the schedule 30 minutes later to allow for the extra rehearsal time you need. It is very likely that the process will feel rushed and stressful.
2. You will most likely end the rehearsal feeling like there is still more that needs to be accomplished and addressed. Inevitably there will be things that come up, and times that your team walks onto the stage feeling unprepared and set up to do much less than their best.
3. It can be vocally exhausting, especially for the worship leader who is leading both the rehearsal and the service. I've worked with many worship leaders who suffer from chronic vocal fatigue and vocal issues that arose out of this type of rehearsal/service format. It's a marathon, and for many worship leaders and singers, it's not sustainable.

   If you absolutely have to stick with this format because of the schedule and structure of your ministry, doing as much as you can to prepare your team prior to rehearsal can go a long way. Getting lead sheets or music to your singers with recordings of the songs and instructions for the parts you'd like each person to sing can help your team come into rehearsal more prepared.

On the day of the service, I still recommend beginning the rehearsal with the instrumentalists and vocalists separated. During sound check and band setup, the singers can spend some time on the three areas we discussed above for a successful vocal rehearsal. You can also lead the band through some things that won't be critical for the singers. Once the singers return to the mix, take some time to do an adequate vocal sound check, get the monitors up, and then jump into the full rehearsal with band and vocalists.

This may require recruiting and developing someone other than the worship leader to lead the vocal rehearsal. Take the time to meet with this person during the week, before the rehearsal, so that he or she will have all the necessary information to adequately lead the singers in your absence.

The One-Rehearsal Process

This process involves a rehearsal days before the worship service. In this format you can rehearse exclusively with your singers and really focus on the three areas discussed above. I have found that a 90-minute rehearsal is usually best to allow adequate time for all three components of a vocal rehearsal. As long as there is a brief rehearsal with the band that is a part of sound check on the day of the service, I don't believe there is any need for the singers to join the band until that day.

The Two-Rehearsal Process

In my experience, this is the ideal rehearsal structure for singers in a worship environment. Usually this isn't necessary for the band, but the singers play a different role. Because it provides the space and time they need to really prepare their voices and their hearts to lead worship, this is a great format.

In this format the first rehearsal (more than a week before the service) can be dedicated solely to the first two components we've talked about: nail down the harmonies and rehearse the structure of the song. Then, in the second rehearsal, you can touch briefly on the musical components, spending the majority of the rehearsal on the heart. Sixty minutes is usually adequate for each of these rehearsals.

The benefit of this structure is the time it gives the singers to allow the song (both musically and lyrically) to saturate their minds, voices, and hearts. They know the music and they are prepared! This frees them up to bring the best of their vocal ability and to move beyond preoccupation with notes and words in order to truly lead from the heart in worship.

This process requires a great deal of preparation from the leadership, but gaining the full benefit from this structure also requires a commitment from every singer in the ministry.

They must be dedicated to doing their homework between rehearsal one and rehearsal two. The expectation for that second rehearsal should be that they walk in the door with their parts nailed and words memorized! Your commitment to them is to show up prepared and ready to provide them with everything they need in that first rehearsal. Their commitment to you is to take that and run with it and come to the second rehearsal ready to get into the good stuff!

Get Rid of Music Stands!

Ideally, you should have this as a goal regardless of your rehearsal process, but certainly if you are in a two-rehearsal process there is no reason why your singers should require music stands. Music stands act like the Grand Canyon between the singers on our worship team and our congregation—they are a huge physical barrier. If singers have music stands in front of them they'll use them, whether they need the notes and words or not. Their faces and eyes will be buried in their stands, their attention focused on the notes and words—distracting them from fully engaging and expressing their hearts in worship, and depriving the congregation of experiencing communication that is inviting and contagious.

If this is a change for your team, be prepared for some serious wailing and gnashing of teeth. Your team will probably cry out like Linus when Lucy has taken his blanket away. Stick to your guns on this one. There is no reason why every intelligent adult can't memorize a worship set. I was reminded of this when I visited my undergraduate alma mater a few years back and saw a performance of the men's choral group I had been a part of during my four years as a student. About sixty 18- to 22-year-old "kids" got onto the stage and for an hour and a half sang complex choral repertoire that spanned five languages and about 400 years of composition. And all of it was memorized. A 20-minute worship set, with predictable harmonies that are all structured around a three- or four-chord progression, is hardly difficult music. The lyrics in our worship choruses are simple, in the language we speak all day long, and often repetitive. Your team will get used to this new challenge, and the effectiveness of their worship leading will take a huge step forward.

Community

It is important to nurture a sense of community between the singers in your worship ministry. It is very easy for us to get busy with life, and even in the context of ministry we can be so focused on the task at hand that people can come in and out the doors of our church, attend rehearsals, lead services, and not really know anyone personally (or be known) over the course of their involvement. Some of this relationship building can take place in the course of rehearsals and serving together with some of the ideas mentioned earlier, but you can do more to help foster community on your team.

Team Meetings

I think it's a great idea for all of the singers (and even the instrumentalists and tech teams, depending on the size of your ministry) to gather for a quarterly meeting. Hold the meeting off campus at the home of someone on your team with a house large enough to host everyone. This provides a casual environment for your team to gather, and it gives you as the leader some extended time with your team without the usual pressures of the task at hand bearing down. Use this meeting as a chance to welcome new team members, share some vision for the ministry, and, most importantly, to give the members of your team the chance to get to know each other on a deeper level. You may want to spend part of your time with them split into smaller groups, and have some exercises or discussion questions that will help facilitate conversations that get below the surface.

Outings

Get together and have some fun! Go take over a karaoke bar on a Friday night, or have a crazy dress-up theme and go bowling! Ministry can be demanding and intense, and it's good to get together to laugh and play, for no other reason than it's fun!

Retreats

One of the things we would do as a vocal ministry every year when I first joined the team at Willow Creek was to get away one weekend a year for a retreat. We would bring in an outside guest worship leader to lead all of the music for our services so that nobody had to stay home (even staff). This allowed all of us to get away as a team. It was always a rich time of spiritual growth, beautiful community building, and lighthearted fun and laughter.

The Importance of Development

At Willow Creek, the most successful singer in our ministry was the most dedicated, hardworking singer I have ever met in my life. He had accomplished more than any of us, having sung in countless professional studio sessions for film, radio, and television. He had his own album, and you could hear his voice on many others. He was also extremely humble, so unless you really badgered him, he'd never tell you about the amazing gig he'd just gotten that week. If any of us on the team had the right to kick back and coast, it was this guy. He already functioned on a level that most of us would never attain. And yet he worked harder and more consistently than any of us, keeping his voice in shape and building it to the next level. He had taken master's level pedagogy classes and decades of voice lessons, and if you asked him at any given time what he was currently working on with his voice and trying to develop, he could give you a detailed description, because that's exactly what he was doing, all the time: constantly developing the best in the gifts and talents that he had been given.

He set the bar, the standard for the entire ministry. It was just a given that we were all expected to be in a constant state of development. It wasn't okay to coast and stagnate. You'd get called on it.

It Starts at the Top

Establishing your ministry as a place that values artistic development is one of the most important characteristics of a healthy ministry. We should always be striving to get better, always looking to deliver our absolute best. And that value starts at the top. It does no good to preach the importance of development and growth if you, as the leader, aren't actively refining your skills and developing your talent. The most successful ministries I know are led by leaders who are always in a process of development, expanding the gifts and abilities they've been given. Take lessons, go to vocal training conferences, set goals, and dedicate yourself to the work of vocal development.

Develop the Gifts Around You

If you truly value development and want to see every one of your singers working on developing his or her voice, you need to be prepared to assist them in the process, as most singers aren't sure where to begin. But the reality for most worship leaders is that you already feel like you're doing your best to keep your head above water just keeping pace with weekly services and special holiday events! I've spent fifteen years as a full-time staff member at churches and I was always amazed that Sunday kept coming around once a week—it's a lot to keep up with!

I am not suggesting that you need to be the one doing the coaching and development. You don't have the time, and many worship leaders find that that's not where their gifts are. What you need to do, though, is to be prepared to refer your singers to resources and opportunities that will allow them to develop their gifts. Research local vocal instructors, and maybe even take a few lessons yourself to make sure that the teaching is sound and that the instructor understands the stylistic target you and your singers will be shooting for. Make sure that you are sending your team members to an instructor who can help them develop in the direction you need them to grow. Many vocal coaches won't really be equipped (or interested) to help your team work on the style or techniques presented in this book. If you can't find local instructors who are going to be a great fit for your ministry, there are opportunities online where singers can get individual instruction. Find other resources, such as training CDs and DVDs that will help singers to develop their voices. You may also want to consider bringing in a vocal coach for a weekend seminar, providing a concentrated experience for your singers to light a fire and motivate them to work on developing their full potential. If you're not sure where to start, check out www.VocalArtistry.com for a full listing of services and resources.

Value People

Developing the gifts of the people around you not only serves to build your worship ministry, but it also shows the people on your team that you honor and value them. I have seen singers discarded from a ministry because they weren't measuring up or because their style was becoming last year's model. Sometimes changes and transitions need to happen, particularly if a singer in your ministry is digging in his or her heels and showing reluctance to move, grow, and develop in the direction that the ministry is transitioning. But many singers have amazing openness to grow and change; they just need an opportunity to build and develop their gifts. Don't just discard these singers! Find people with heart and passion and commitment and build into them. Flashy talent is easy to find, and a singer with great talent and a sour heart can end up tearing your ministry apart. Singers who are committed for the long haul, dedicated to growth and development, and committed to the values of your team are the singers who will provide a solid foundation for you to build your ministry around.

Along those same lines, be sure to honor seasoned veterans. As style changes, ministries grow, and as singers age, you may see a singer's role change on your team. Too often, however, these singers are alienated from the ministry they have served, sometimes for decades, or, even worse, discarded and replaced with the new upcoming talent. Seasoned veterans have a lot to offer the young people on your team. Their experience and maturity can provide a cornerstone for your ministry to build upon. Find ways to keep them involved, and help them develop and grow. With the right tools in place, you may be amazed at how adaptable their skills really are, and they will offer a depth to your ministry that you will never find in new, young talent.

About the DVD-ROM

Welcome!

The video and audio material on this DVD-ROM build on the information presented in *The Worship Vocal Book*. The videos provide a tour of your instrument and illustrate the techniques and stylistic tools presented in the text. The audio content presents vocal exercises specifically designed to help you begin a workout program to develop your voice.

Video Content

1. Tour of the Larynx

The larynx is the most amazing instrument on planet earth! This segment will take you on a tour of the larynx, introducing you to the main structures of the instrument we play (thyroid cartilage, cricoid cartilage, arytenoid cartilages, and vocal cords) and their basic function.

2. Breathing Technique

Understanding the way our body is designed to breathe is important in order to develop a technique that will allow us to use the full capacity of our lungs. This tutorial will offer a description and visual explanation of the

- Diaphragm
- Intercostal muscles
- Abdominal muscles
- Breathing technique

3. Support Demonstration

All of the energy for our voice is provided by breath support. This tutorial will demonstrate how to engage the diaphragm for maximum energy and support.

4. Style Demo: Diction

The way that we form vowels and articulate consonants significantly affects our vocal style. This tutorial will demonstrate how we use diction differently in modern worship compared to classical/choral style.

5. Style Demo: Tone Color

There are many ways we can alter the tone of our voice in order to provide stylistic color and nuance. This segment will demonstrate the different tones we use most often in modern worship.

6. Style Demo: Vibrato

The use of vibrato is an important tool in helping us to express our heart as we sing. This segment will demonstrate the effect that different uses of vibrato have on a song.

7. Style Demo: Pitch Bends

Use of vocal pitch bending significantly affects our delivery of stylistic inflections and emotion. This segment demonstrates not only how to use pitch bends in modern worship, but also how and when to avoid them.

8. Microphone Technique

The microphone is part of the instrument you play as a singer in modern worship. This tutorial will demonstrate how to hold a mic and how to get the most out of it as you sing.

Audio Content

1. Neck Tension Exercise

This exercise is designed to alleviate tension in the neck. As you perform the exercise, slowly roll your head from side to side in order to keep the neck muscles loose and relaxed.

2. Jaw Tension Exercise

Perform this exercise as you massage the hinge of your jaw to keep the jaw relaxed and free from tension. Allow the jaw to hang loose, without moving as you change vowels.

3. Laryngeal Tension Exercise

On this exercise, monitor the position of the larynx and yawn the throat as open as possible to keep it down.

4. Lip, Face, and Cheek Tension Exercise

Also referred to as the "lip-buzz exercise," this exercise is performed while the lips vibrate as they would if you were blowing bubbles in a swimming pool.

5. Tongue Tension Exercise

Hold your tongue out of your mouth with the help of a Handi Wipe on this exercise. Make sure that you sing this song on a wide-open "ah" vowel as in "father," and not "a" as in "apple."

6. Breathing Exercise

Relax the abdomen, allowing your stomach to expand as you take the breath in, and then to tighten back in as you sing out. This exercise will help you to develop the coordination for the breathing technique described in the text, and teach you to expand your lungs to their full capacity.

7. Support Exercise

Support for the voice is achieved as we internally push down and out against the constriction of the abdominal muscles while we sing. This exercise will help you to feel this coordination and get more energy for your singing.

8. Octave Yodel Exercise 1

Welcome to the Grand Ole Opry! On this exercise the goal is to yodel every time you change pitch and switch between head voice and chest voice (and vice versa). If you sound good on this exercise, with a smooth transition between pitches, you're doing it completely wrong. You'll know you've got it right if you sound like a donkey and your voice cracks between every pitch you sing.

9. Octave Yodel Exercise 2

Hold on tight! This exercise uses the same idea as the previous exercise, only at twice the speed.

10. Isolated Head Voice Exercise (Women)

This exercise is a great workout for the head voice for women. Keep your lips puckered on an "oo" vowel as if you're sipping through a straw. The tone should be light and floaty.

11. Isolated Chest Voice Exercise (Women)

On this exercise you will shout between each scale that you sing. Using the shout as a reference point, keep the same tone as you sing the scale.

12. Isolated Head Voice Exercise (Men)

This exercise is a great workout for the head voice for men. Keep your lips puckered on an "oo" vowel as if you're sipping through a straw. The tone should be light and floaty.

13. Isolated Chest Voice Exercise (Men)

On this exercise, use the fullest and most open tone possible. The goal is a rich, classical sound.

14. Chest Blend Exercise (Women)

This exercise should be sung in a predominantly chest-voice production, without flipping over into head voice. In order to get a chest blend instead of using full chest voice on this exercise, sing with increased nasality; use a narrow projection that makes it feel as if you are sending your voice to a specific point, and sing a bit more softly than you do in pure chest voice. Be careful not to strain your voice on this exercise; only sing as high as you can comfortably and then stop.

15. Chest Blend Exercise (Men)

This exercise should be sung in a predominantly chest-voice production, without flipping over into head voice. In order to get a chest blend instead of using full chest voice on this exercise, sing with increased nasality; use a narrow projection that makes it feel as if you are sending your voice to a specific point, and sing a bit more softly than you do in pure chest voice. Be careful not to strain your voice on this exercise; only sing as high as you can comfortably and then stop.

Index

Worship Musician!™ PRESENTS Series

Tips for Tight Teams

High-Performance Help
for Today's Worship Musician

by Sandy Hoffman
Hal Leonard

Tips for Tight Teams instructs and equips today's worship musician to function on the musical, relational, and technical levels expected of 21st-century worship team leaders and members. Rooted in Sandy Hoffman's "Ten Top Tips for Tight Teams" curriculum, the book covers a myriad of timeless and relevant worship topics. The goal of *Tips for Tight Teams* is to elevate skill levels to the point where the worship team is no longer a distraction to the people it endeavors to lead into worship.

$16.99 • 8-1/2" x 11" • 160 pages • Softcover
978-1-4584-0291-2

Photography in Worship

The Art and Science of Iconic Imagery

by Mike Overlin
Hal Leonard

The ability to take a photograph – to stop a moment in time – is a very powerful act in and of itself. When this skill is used in the creation of imagery in support of worship, or even as an act of worship, it can be truly breathtaking. This book will teach you the basics of photography through simple explanations and practical examples, and more important, how to "see" the image in advance, with special emphasis on creating imagery for use in worship.

$29.99 • 8-1/2" x 11" • 208 pages • Softcover
978-1-4584-0295-0

The Worship Band Book

Training and Empowering
Your Worship Band

by Tom Lane
Hal Leonard

Whether you're in a band yourself or part of a ministry involved with teams, this book can help you on your journey. Spiritual, relational, professional, and practical issues relevant for individuals and groups in worship ministry of any kind are addressed head-on. This book will help lay the foundation for a healthier pursuit of creative dreams and a closer walk with God.

$16.99 • 8-1/2" x 11" • 128 pages • Softcover
978-1-4584-1817-3

HAL•LEONARD®

Prices, contents, and availability subject to change without notice.